Is

God

Dead?

Is God Dead?

by Richard Wolff

TYNDALE HOUSE, PUBLISHERS

WHEATON, ILLINOIS

CONTENTS

chapter 1

A New Gospel

When a concept as radical as "God is dead" is seriously debated by theologians, animatedly discussed in churches and on college campuses, and even repeated by wide-eyed children, it is time for responsible men and women to take a hard, close look at the phenomenon.

The idea that "God is dead" is not new; why should the slogan generate so much interest today? What triggers such a movement—if it is a movement? What is the real impact of such a pronouncement? Does the cry "God is dead" rise from a significant segment of society? Is it typical of the contemporary mood or indicative of things to come? Is it as radical as it sounds? To answer the last question first, examine these declarations:

"All established theological language, whether of conservative or liberal orientation, is receding into meaninglessness, irrelevance or banality."[1]

"Given our historical situation in the twilight of Christendom, we have long since died to the possibility of a classical or orthodox Christian belief, and we must look upon both the New Testament and early Christianity as exotic and alien forms of religion."[2]

"The greatest theological problem of our time is an understanding of the meaning of the death of God."[3]

"Contemporary theology is unquestionably in a state of

crisis, perhaps the most profound crisis which Christian theology has faced since its creation."[4]

"The essentially mythological worldview of Christianity has been succeeded by a thorough scientific view of reality, in terms of which either God is no longer necessary, or he is neither necessary nor unnecessary: he is irrelevant—he is dead."[5]

These stunning statements were not made by humanistic scientists nor atheistic Communists, but by theologians who call themselves Christians. "God is dead," they announce unequivocally, and listeners frown, wince, or tremble. What do these men mean? How can religious leaders preach that "God is dead?" Where did this bizarre idea come from?

Some 80 years ago the German philosopher Friedrich Nietzsche wrote: "The greatest recent event—that 'God is dead,' that the belief in the Christian God has ceased to be believable—is even now beginning to cast its first shadows over Europe....In the main, however, this may be said: the event itself is much too great, too distant, too far from the comprehension of the many even for the tidings of it to be thought of as having *arrived* yet, not to speak of the notion that many people might know what has really happened here, and what must collapse now that this belief has been undermined—all that was built upon it, leaned on it, grew into it: for example, our whole European morality...."[6]

Nietzsche also pictured a madman "who lit a lantern in the bright morning hours, ran to the market place, and cried incessantly, 'I seek God! I seek God!' " As many who did not believe in God were standing around, the madman provoked much laughter. " 'Whither is God?' he cried. 'I shall tell you. *We have killed him*—you and I. All of us are his murderers ....Are we not straying as through an infinite nothing? Do we not feel the breath of an empty space? Has it not become colder? Is not night and more night coming on all the while? ...God is dead. God remains dead....' At last he [i.e. the madman] threw his lantern on the ground, and it broke and went out. 'I come too early,' he said to them; 'my time has not come yet.' This tremendous event is still on its way, still wandering—it has not yet reached the ears of man."[7]

Nietzsche assumed that the dreadful news of the death of God would take a few more centuries to permeate Europe, but two generations later Thomas J. J. Altizer, professor of Bible and Religion at Emory University in Georgia, assumed the truth of the Nietzschean proclamation and announced the new gospel. What had happened in the 60-year interval, especially in the decade of the '50s, to inspire such a revolutionary proclamation in the '60s?

The answer is given in no uncertain terms: Man has "come of age"; the scientific atmosphere, technological progress and the phenomenon of urbanization have made it mandatory to proclaim that "God is dead." The orthodox concept of a personal God is inadequate, no longer serviceable. A scientific worldview leaves no option but to affirm the death of God. The most radical of theological views has now become necessary and natural.

Theologians Rudolf Bultmann and Paul Tillich did not go far enough, say the radical theologians. The neo-orthodox and existential theologians failed to recognize the great event —the death of God. It is said that we must go beyond the "nonbeing of God" described by Tillich and the "hiddenness of God" defined by Bultmann.

The dilemma facing modern theologians is summarized by Union Seminary's John Macquarrie: "How can we think of God? How can we talk about him? There was a time when questions like these might have been absurd, for most people did talk about God and believed that they had a sufficiently clear conception of what they meant when they talked about him. The idea of God was part of the apparatus in terms of which people thought about themselves and their world, and so the word 'God' communicated when it was uttered. Communication depends on the sharing of basic ideas and presuppositions which allow one person's discourse to be intelligible to another person.

"But let us suppose that some of these presuppositions

11

are gradually eroded away, and that new modes of thinking about ourselves and the world take their place. Then some words that once communicated may not communicate any longer. We find that we cannot place them within the framework of our thinking. They become increasingly vague and indeterminate, and may end up without any assignable meaning at all. Something like this has happened to the word 'God' in our own time."[8]

Bultmann, Tillich, Dietrich Bonhoeffer, and Jewish theologian Martin Buber tried to solve the problem, each in his own way. "Ultimate concern," "ultimate reality," the " 'Beyond' in our midst," "encounter," the "I-Thou" mode are samples of their solutions. But the self-styled radicals are dissatisfied with these suggestions; they proclaim with dogmatic assurance that "God is dead."

Actually, the "God is dead" school comprises only a few men. Though they differ among themselves in details, they agree that the concept of a personal God, Creator and Redeemer can no longer be held. Nietzsche's dictum is beyond all controversy, they assert, and must be accepted without further debate.

In his book, *The Gospel of Christian Atheism,* Altizer names the mystical poet William Blake (and philosopher G. W. F. Hegel, along with Nietzsche as his theological forebears. Since "modern man" allegedly cannot accept the theological world-picture of the New Testament, and the New Testament and early Christianity are alien religious forms to contemporary man, the Christian Scriptures must be discarded in favor of philosophers and mystics. For the radical theologians the "good news" of Christianity is that "God is dead," and this message must be joyfully proclaimed to all men!

Is this ingenious inspiration? Magnificent delusion? Exotic heresy? What is really meant by the expression, "God is dead?"

1. Altizer, T. J. J., "Creative Negation in Theology," *Christian Century,* July 7, 1965, p. 864.
2. Altizer, T. J. J., *The Gospel of Christian Atheism* (Philadelphia: The Westminster Press), 1966, p. 105.
3. Altizer, T. J. J., "Word and History," *Theology Today,* Vol. XXII, No. 3, October, 1965, pp. 380-393.

4. Altizer, T. J. J. and Hamilton, William, *Radical Theology and the Death of God* (New York: The Bobbs-Merrill Co., Inc.), 1966, p. 95.
5. Vahanian, Gabriel, *The Death of God* (New York: George Braziller), 1961, p. XXXII.
6. *The Gay Science*, Bk. X (343).
7. Ibid., No. 125.
8. "How Can We Think of God?" Martin E. Marty and Dean G. Peerman's *New Theology No.* 3 (New York: The Macmillan Company), 1966, p. 40.

chapter 2

What Do They Mean?

How is the slogan "God is dead" defined? Does it mean that God has ceased to exist? Or is the idea of God irrelevant to modern man because his problems are purely secular? Has science made supernatural faith impossible? Is it no longer necessary to place confidence in a superior Being because man has come of age? Or does it simply mean that for all practical purposes most people live without God?

GABRIEL VAHANIAN

The name of Gabriel Vahanian is often associated with the "God-is-dead" theologians, especially because of the title of his book *The Death of God*. Vahanian, professor at Syracuse University, defines the death of God as the absence of God experienced by man, an absence which is no longer a theoretical declaration but a practical awareness.[1]

Vahanian should not be classified among the "God-is-dead" theologians in a strict sense. Writer Ved Mehta reported that theologian Langdon Gilkey planned a book on the movement dealing with Hamilton, Altizer, and Van Buren, and Vahanian was considered to be too conservative.[2]

When Vahanian addressed a convocation at Indiana State University, he admitted in the panel discussion following his lecture that the title of his book does not mean that God is really dead. He indicated that "the death of God" is only a useful phrase to underscore that today the church as an organization no longer controls politics as the medieval church did.[3] Similarly, in his book *Wait Without Idols*, Vahanian indicated that the expression "God is dead" should not be interpreted to mean that God himself no longer exists, but that his reality as the Christian tradition has presented it has become culturally irrelevant.[4] Throughout, Vahanian is concerned with cultural realities rather than theological considerations.

Vahanian's book presents a thoughtful diagnosis of the contemporary scene and summarizes his basic findings in three concluding statements:

(1) Christianity today is synonymous with religiosity. Its appeal to the masses is based on a diluted version of the original faith; the radical character of biblical faith is diluted into religiosity, purely formal, innocuous, somewhat hygienic.

(2) We live in a post-Christian era because our culture is gradually losing the marks of that Christianity which brought it into being and shaped it. Christianity is no longer coextensive with our culture. "Christianity was instrumental in setting up the foundations of modern science and all that derives from it in the fields of technology or even sociology and economics."[5]

(3) We now live in a post-Christian era in which tolerance has become religious syncretism, an amalgam of beliefs and attitudes without content or backbone.[6] The novelty, or tragedy, of our situation lies in the fact that our age is post-Christian both theologically and culturally.

Vahanian concludes: "If we can no longer assume that God is, we may once again realize that He *must* be. God is not necessary, but He is inevitable. He is wholly other and wholly present. Faith in him, the conversion of our human reality, both culturally and existentially, is a demand he still makes upon us, the choice he confronts us with."[7]

Paul M. Van Buren

Paul Van Buren is associate professor of theology at Episcopal Theological Seminary of the Southwest in Austin,

Texas. He says that the Absolute has "died of neglect"; "a quiet displacement has taken place" by a "different habit of thought" which now prevails.[8]

"Today, we cannot even understand the Nietzschean cry that 'God is dead!' " he says, "for if it were so, how could we know? No, the problem is that the *word* 'God' is dead."[9] The word "God" has become meaningless to modern man. We no longer have an "ultimate concern," or at least, "care must be exercised in speaking of the 'ultimate concern' " and for that matter of all absolutes such as "absolute commitment" or "unique revelation."

Secularism is the dominant note. Van Buren uses the word "secular" to designate certain empirical attitudes: "Call it a deep interest in questions of human life this side of the 'beyond,' and a corresponding lack of interest in what were once felt to be great metaphysical questions."[10]

Van Buren believes that God is no longer part of the "network of forces and factors of everyday existence." God is no longer considered the cause of "real" phenomena, such as death, life, rain, etc. Van Buren applies the word "real" to describe our "agreement about how things are, according to certain ground rules." Since Van Buren excludes God from these ground rules, God is ipso facto excluded from "reality." But the ground rules are a matter of individual conviction. To the Christian, God is not only part of the ground rules but at the very heart of "reality."

Van Buren suggests that we may suffer from a "monistic hangover"—that many people are looking for one unifying factor to embrace a great, coherent system. He feels that this is no longer possible. We must be relativists and live with a plurality of values and understandings. Truth and falsehood depend on the particular point of reference. Van Buren asserts it is pointless to raise a question regarding the existence of "some absolute being, even 'Being itself,' which is 'behind' or 'beyond' all we know and are, some final ground and end of all created things." In the face of such questions, counsels Van Buren, the Christian "will be wise to remain silent."[11]

In the Introduction to his book *The Secular Meaning of the Gospel,* Van Buren repeats a parable told by Anthony Flew, a British philosopher. "Once upon a time," goes the story, "two explorers came upon a clearing in the jungle. In the clearing were growing many flowers and many weeds. One explorer said, 'Some gardener must tend this plot.' The other disagrees: 'There is no gardener.' So they pitched their tents and set a watch.

"No gardener is ever seen. 'But perhaps he is an invisible gardener,' they speculated. So they set up a barbed wire fence. They electrified it. They patroled with bloodhounds. But no shrieks ever betray the presence of an intruder. No movement of the wire reveals an invisible climber. The bloodhounds never bay an alarm. Yet the Believer is adamant: 'There *is* a gardener, invisible, intangible, insensible to electric shocks, a gardener who has no scent and makes no sound, a gardener who comes secretly to look after the garden which he loves.' The Skeptic gibes, 'But what is left of your original assertion? Just how does what you call an invisible, intangible, eternally elusive gardener differ from an imaginary gardener or no gardener at all?'"

Then Flew concludes, "A fine, brash hypothesis may thus be killed by inches, the death of a thousand qualifications."

A God who is never operative in human affairs, who is totally silent, completely absent, eternally hidden, such a God is "dead," says this parable of Flew's. The doctrine of God has died bit by bit through a thousand qualifications when his personality is denied, his revelation rejected, when everything supernatural and objective is negated. Indeed, nothing is left of God, and there is nothing to believe in. Nothing is left of the original faith in a living God who manifests himself in history.

The Christian viewpoint is that the gardener did enter into the garden, God was in Christ reconciling the world. Christ said: He who has seen me has seen the Father. A denial of the resurrection leads inevitably to the conclusion of Flew's parable.

William Hamilton, professor of systematic theology at Colgate Rochester Divinity School, found himself in a spiritual dilemma in 1965 which he tentatively resolved. In an interview with Ved Mehta, Hamilton said, "A lot of people nowadays 'make it' without believing in God, and without despairing about not believing in God, so God may be dead or gone. But I am still waiting or hoping for God to rise up again. However, I am beginning to feel that the time has come for me to put up or shut up, for me to be an *in* or an *out*."[12]

Later, speaking of the death of God, he wrote: "I am not here referring to a belief in the non-existence of God. . . . When we speak of the death of God, we speak not only of the death of the idols or the falsely objectivized Being in the sky; we speak, as well, of the death in us of any power to affirm any of the traditional images of God. I mean that the world is not God and that it does not point to God."[13]

More explicitly, Hamilton states: "We are not talking about the absence of the experience of God, but about the experience of the absence of God."[14] He adds: "My Protestant faith has no God, has no faith in God, and affirms both the death of God and the death of all forms of theism."

In *Thursday's Child*—perhaps a thinly disguised autobiographical note—the theologian discovers that at the center of his thoughts and meditation is a void, a disappearance, an absence. At the same time, paradoxically, the concept of "waiting" for God is advanced, maintaining an element of expectation and allowing a glimmer of hope. Although God is not necessary since the world is a sufficient need-fulfiller, God may perhaps be enjoyed and delighted in, Hamilton concedes. So a certain "waiting" for God may be permitted, thus differentiating the Christian from the conventional atheist and removing the gloom and anguish typical of atheism. The radical Christian thus stands before God in unbelief and seeks out ways in which the unnecessary and unneeded God may be enjoyed.[15]

Hamilton echoes Bonhoeffer when he expresses the feeling

that the religious premise of man has disappeared, and he claims that there is no way—cultural, ontological or psychological—to locate a part of the self or of human experience that needs God. There is no God-shaped blank within man. Contrary to Augustine's assertion, man's heart may or may not be restless till it rests in God. God is only one of the many possibilities in a radically pluralistic environment.

By way of a provisional summary, Hamilton concludes that the death of God must be affirmed. But our waiting for God, our godlessness, is partly a search for language and a style to enable us to stand before him once again, delighting in his presence.[16]

Hamilton reacts against the God who is viewed as a problem-solver and need-fulfiller. Secular man, man come of age, is unwilling to ask God to do for us what the world is qualified to do. To really travel along this road means that we must trust the world, not God, to be our need-fulfiller and problem-solver, and God, if he is to be for us at all, must come in some other role.[17]

Interestingly, philosopher Karl Jaspers declares: "Man cannot help taking something as an absolute, whether willingly and knowingly, whether accidentally and fitfully or resolutely and steadfastly. Man has a kind of home in the absolute. He cannot evade it. In that home he must live."[18]

THOMAS J. J. ALTIZER

At first sight it would seem that Thomas Altizer, while more radical than the other "radical theologians," is also clearer. He writes: "A radical theology that confesses the death of God is not simply a theological form of atheistic humanism or naturalism. . . . A Christian confession of the death of God is a response to the real absence of God himself. . . . We must speak of the concrete actuality of God's withdrawal from our time. To speak the name of God in a time of his withdrawal is nothing less than blasphemy. . . ."[19]

Altizer emphasizes that God has actually died. This does not mean that modern man "is incapable of believing in God, or that modern culture is an idolatrous flight from the presence of God, or even that we exist in a time when God has chosen to be silent. Nor is it possible to say that these words [i.e. "God is dead"] must mean that the Word of God transcends all human expressions of faith, or that the true God is above the God of metaphysics and religion ...because God has disappeared from history he is no longer present for faith. But he is truly absent, he is not simply hidden from view, and therefore he is truly dead."

Altizer says the death of God is a historical event, "a final and irrevocable event," with all traditional Christian images being lost and transcendence being swallowed up in immanence. "God has died in *our* time, in *our* history, in *our* existence,"[20] declares Altizer.

Altizer cites the historic moment when the death of God occurred. God was once manifest and real as Creator and Lord,[21] but his incarnation in Jesus was a decisive and real event which effected a real change or movement in God himself. God became fully incarnate when he became Jesus, thereby ceasing to exist in his primordial form.[22] The incarnation of God in Jesus is only real, Altizer insists, if it resulted in the death of the original sacred, the death of God himself.[23] Just as the spoken word empties the speaker of himself, so God was emptied by the movement of the incarnation. God's essential being was left behind in an empty, lifeless form, with his incarnate mode of existence being the very opposite of his original being. So God fully and finally ceased to exist in his original form.[24]

Altizer goes further. The preincarnate form of God having become lifeless and immobile, he says, it has gradually regressed to the formless state of an abstract and empty nothingness. This empty nothingness is recognized by fallen humanity as a "Devouring Power" or "Satan."[25] Redemption can only be completed after the transcendent, God has undergone a historical epiphany as Satan.[26] Thus the guilt fostering God has disappeared and mankind is freed.

Altizer analyzes the necessity for God to die from a

different angle as he interprets the theological implications of the Oedipus complex. The human desire to murder one's father is necessary to make possible the freedom of the sons; but as this murder produces a sense of guilt which in turn leads to self-denial, man cannot enjoy the fruit of the patricide and he represses his guilt-feelings. Then the joyful message is proclaimed that repression and guilt feelings may be discarded,[27] for the God who originated repression and induced guilt has been sacrificed to Satan on Calvary, and the atonement has become the abolition of all confinement and repression. Therefore the radical Christian welcomes the death of God, wills the death of God and hails the death of God as a liberating event![28]

Altizer explains the changes in God's manifestations this way: "Once God has died in Christ to his transcendent epiphany, that epiphany must inevitably recede into an abstract and alien form, eventually becoming the full embodiment of every alien other, and thence appearing to consciousness as the ultimate source of all repression. Already we have seen that faith can name this movement as the metamorphosis of God into Satan, as God empties himself of his original power and glory and progressively becomes manifest as an alien but oppressive nothingness.

"We must understand this whole movement as an atoning process, a forward-moving process wherein a vacuous and nameless power of evil becomes increasingly manifest as the dead body of God or Satan; but it is precisely this epiphany of God as Satan which numbs the power of evil, and unveils every alien and oppressive other as a backward-moving regression into the now lifeless and hence ultimately powerless emptiness of the primordial sacrality of God."[29]

God is now seen as a "forwarding moving process"; he is undergoing a perpetual incarnation. God is revealed in a continually changing series of historical moments, unfolding himself in the concrete processes of time and space, here and now. Since God is a *forward* moving process of incarnation the Christian must totally negate the *past*.

The question may be raised why the Christian should not contemplate the God who existed as Lord and Creator, the pre-incarnate God. Why refuse all knowledge of this primordial God and concentrate on the incarnate God—equated with a forward-moving process? Altizer answers that even the remembrance of the original glory and majesty of God roots the Christian in the past, so that a study of the pre-incarnate God is not wholesome.[30] Only the present incarnation of God which occurs wherever there is history and life deserves our attention.[31]

Although "God is dead," Altizer informs us, he is not totally out of the picture. The incarnation which continuously occurs here and now is a movement of *God*. Altizer believes: "A profane destiny may yet provide a way to return to the God who is all in all, not by returning to a moment of the past, but by meeting an epiphany of the past in the present."[32]

Through this dialectical process, the opposites coincide: radical negation becomes radical affirmation; the denial of God leads to an affirmation of God. Finally God rises from the ashes like the proverbial phoenix.

The concept of God as the "coincidence of opposites" is an idea borrowed from Mircea Eliade, to whom Altizer is extensively indebted. This viewpoint is explained as a "paradoxical coming together of sacred and profane, being and non-being, absolute and relative, the eternal and the becoming."[33]

Altizer has borrowed from many sources and believes with Joachim of Floris (1135-1202) that the current age is the third age, the final age of the Spirit, totally different from the revelations given in the Old Testament and the New Testament.

This concept can hardly encourage the atheist who doesn't care to discover God reappearing after all, nor can it inspire the Christian who believes himself related now to a personal, supernatural, benevolent Deity.

What is the reaction of other theologians to the "God-is-dead" concept?

John C. Bennett, president of Union Theological Seminary, protests: "Altizer's thought is extremely complicated and confusing. In place of the God of traditional theology, he has substituted a worldview more akin to Buddhist mysticism than to a secularist atheism, and influenced by aspects of Christian teaching about the Word and Spirit. The world he portrays is unlike that pictured by others who believe in a godless universe."[34]

Edmund Perry, professor of history of religion at Northwestern University, observed: "Patience will perhaps reward us with the appearance of more cogent and systematic expositors of this new faith. In the meantime we are left to marvel that men wish to make a religion out of the death of God and seek to propagate it evangelistically with pastoral care for the souls of men and apologetically with a will to destroy the very religion whose continued existence gives the new religion its only reason for emerging and growing. To the mentality of modern men, the death of God is as much a myth as the life of God. For the Christian for whom the presence of God is a reality of his own experience, the death of God can hardly be a living option."[35]

German neo-orthodox theologian Karl Barth dismissed the "God is dead" theology as a "bad joke" and called its proponents "theological playboys" who have studied "neither the Bible nor the history of theology."[36]

The New York Times, under the heading " 'God Is Dead' Debate Widens," editorialized: "The clearest thing about the small but much-publicized 'God is dead' movement in Protestant theology is its catchy, provocative title. After that, all is subtlety, the specialized technical language of the academy, professional abstruseness and lay bafflement."[37]

Even William Hamilton censures his colleague with mixed praise: "Altizer ultimately prefers the categories of neither Christology nor ethics, but of mysticism...Altizer's vision is an exciting one, logically imprecise, calculated to make empiricists weep, but imaginatively and religiously it is both sophisticated and powerful."[38]

Altizer confesses himself to be a disciple of Mircea Eliade whom he calls "the greatest living interpreter of the whole world of primitive and archaic religion, of alchemy in both East and West, and of the various forms of Indian Yoga."[39]

Altizer hardly exaggerates when he states that his concept of the death of God has opened a whole new meaning of creation and incarnation, an interpretation almost unheard of previously except in the circles of mystical or heretical writers.

Apparently the radical theologians have neither satisfied atheists nor been of help to Christians! To the former, God-talk in any form is archaic, and the latter are not willing to negate their experience of the living God in favor of a fanciful theory about a dead God. Relevance, a prime goal of the radical theologians, has not been achieved.

1. *The Death of God, op. cit.,* p. 187.
2. Mehta, Ved, "The New Theologians," *The New Yorker,* Vol. XLI, No. 39, November 13, 1965, p. 142.
3. "God Only Half Dead?" *Christianity Today,* June 10, 1966, p. 29.
4. Vahanian, Gabriel, *Wait Without Idols* (New York: George Braziller), 1964, pp. 31, 32.
5. *The Death of God, op. cit.,* p. 172.
6. *Ibid.,* pp. 49, 40, 228, 229.
7. *Wait Without Idols, op. cit.,* p. 46.
8. "The Dissolution of the Absolute," *Religion in Life,* Vol. XXXIV, Summer, 1965, pp. 334-342.
9. Van Buren, Paul M., *The Secular Meaning of the Gospel* (New York: The Macmillan Co.), 1963, p. 103.
10. *Ibid.,* Preface p. XIV.
11. *Ibid.,* p. 144.
12. "The New Theologians," *op. cit.,* p. 142.
13. Hamilton, William, *The New Essence of Christianity* (New York: Association Press), 1966, pp. 55, 58.
14. *Radical Theology and the Death of God, op. cit.,* pp. 28, 37.
15. *Ibid.,* pp. 41, 90, 117.
16. *Ibid.,* pp.. 40, 41.
17. *Ibid.,* p. 40.
18. Jaspers, Karl, *Way to Wisdom* (New Haven: Yale University Press), 1962, p. 80.
19. "Creative Negation in Theology," *op. cit.,* pp. 864-867.
20. Altizer, T. J. J., *Mircea Eliade and the Dialectic of the Sacred* (Philadelphia: The Westminster Press), 1963, p. 13.
21. *The Gospel of Christian Atheism, op. cit.,* p. 90.
22. *Ibid.,* p. 44.
23. *Ibid.,* p. 54.
24. *Ibid.,* p. 68.
25. *Ibid.,* p. 100.
26. *Ibid.,* p. 96, 97.
27. *Mircea Eliade and the Dialectic of the Sacred, op. cit.,* p. 160 ff.

28. *The Gospel of Christian Atheism, op. cit.,* pp. 145, 146.
29. *Ibid.,* pp. 112-113.
30. *Ibid.,* p. 133.
31. *Ibid.,* p. 43.
32. *Radical Theology and the Death of God, op. cit.,* p. 19.
33. *Mircea Eliade and the Dialectic of the Sacred,* op. cit., p. 16.
34. Bennett, John C., "In Defense of God," *op. cit.,* p. 69.
35. Perry, Edmund, " 'God is Dead'—Their Creed," *Chicago Tribune Books Today,* May 1, 1966, p. 6.
36. *Christianity Today,* May 13, 1966.
37. Cogley, John, " 'God is Dead' Debate Widens," *The New York Times,* January 9, 1966.
38. *Radical Theology and the Death of God, op. cit.,* pp. 30, 31.
39. *Mircea Eliade and the Dialectic of the Sacred, op. cit.,* pp. 20, 16.

chapter 3

Who Is Who?

One of the luminaries on the theological horizon seems to shine on the camps of both orthodox Christianity and the "radical theology." While countless Christians praise the deep devotion to Christ of Dietrich Bonhoeffer, the radical theologians also enlist his aid. William Hamilton, for example, says that his own essay *The Essence of Christianity* is "deeply indebted to Bonhoeffer, and may be taken as a theological response to the coming of age of the world as he [Bonhoeffer] has analyzed it."

DIETRICH BONHOEFFER

The ambiguity about Bonhoeffer stems from the incomplete writings of this German pastor-theologian who was imprisoned and executed for his anti-Nazi activities. His writings and his heroism earned him fame after his death in 1945.

Bonhoeffer did raise the question of how the Gospel could be proclaimed to self-assured modern man, who seemingly has learned to cope with all important questions without recourse to God. It seemed to Bonhoeffer that in all human affairs, what we call "God" is being more and more edged out of life, losing more and more ground. If one suggests that man still needs God in the face of "ultimate" questions such as guilt and death, Bonhoeffer asks what will we do if one day such questions no longer exist and man becomes radically without religion?

"We are proceeding towards a time of no religion at all," predicted Bonhoeffer. "Men as they are now simply cannot be religious anymore...our whole 100-year-old Christian preaching and theology rests upon the "religious premise" of man.... But if one day it becomes apparent that this *a priori* 'premise' simply does not exist...if we reach a stage of being radically without religion—and I think this is more or less the case already, else how is it, for instance, that this war, unlike any other of those before it, is not calling forth any 'religious' reaction—what does that mean for 'Christianity'?"[1]

Bonhoeffer made the meaning of the word "religion" objectionable by definition and then proclaimed a "religionless" Christianity. For example, he compared Paul's question as to whether the circumcision ritual of the Jews is a condition of justification with the question of "religion" as a condition of salvation.[2]

Bonhoeffer deplored the fact that "religious people speak of God when human perception is (often just from laziness) at an end, or human resources fail: it is really always the *Deus ex machina* they call to their aid, either for the so-called solving of insoluble problems or as support in human failure—always, that is to say, helping out human weakness or on the borders of human existence."[3]

In other words, religious people often use God as a stopgap, especially in an extreme situation. Or the "religious" person believes that God is at his beck and call, Bonhoeffer charges, defining such a religion as "morbidly personal." Bonhoeffer was convinced that God should not be "used" that way, that he should not merely represent the way out of an impasse, or be conceived as the one who delivers out of an extreme situation when all else has failed.

If man learns to cope with most of his problems, Bonhoeffer posits, does God then become superfluous for those who seek him only on the "borders of human existence?" Bonhoeffer's answer is that it is not necessary for the Christian to frantically "make room" for God. Rather, says Bonhoeffer, God "must be found at the center of life.... Christ is the center of life, and in no sense did he come to answer our unsolved problems."

Do Dietrich Bonhoeffer's writings fit the pattern of the "God is dead" school? Though some of his statements appear self-contradictory and obscure, Bonhoeffer states his conviction clearly: "I should like to speak of God not on the borders of life but at its center, not in weakness but in strength, not, therefore, in man's suffering and death but in his life and prosperity."[4] He defines "religionless Christianity" as the faith in God who is the "beyond" in the midst of life. He adds: "The church stands not where human powers give out, not on the borders, but in the center of the village."

It is important also to understand Bonhoeffer's concept of worldliness." His viewpoint is well-illuminated by his observation that Martin Luther lived a "this-worldly life." The Christian should live completely in this world and abandon every attempt to merely play a role. "This is what I mean by worldliness—taking life in one's stride, with all its duties and problems, its successes and failures, its experiences and helplessness. It is in such a life that we throw ourselves utterly in the arms of God...."[5] No escape-mechanism, no retreat, no religious jargon, a keen sense of responsibility and concrete involvement, this is living a genuine Christian life in a world "come of age." He speaks of "an abandonment of a false conception of God, and a clearing of the decks for the God of the Bible."[6]

Bonhoeffer's proclamation of Jesus Christ is unequivocal as he writes of a faith which sets life upon a new foundation. "This foundation is the life, the death and the resurrection of the Lord Jesus Christ. Without this foundation a life is unjustified before God. It is delivered up to death and damnation....Faith means the finding and holding fast of this foundation. It means casting anchor upon it and being held fast by it. Faith means founding my life upon a foundation which is outside myself, upon an eternal and holy foundation, upon Christ, no longer seeing anything but him, being wrested from my imprisonment in my own self, being set free by Jesus Christ."[7]

Further, he writes: "Jesus does not call men to a new religion, but to life."[8] When God is presented in a "non-religious" way, the ungodliness of the world must not be glossed over, but be exposed in a new light. It must become clear, says Bonhoeffer, that "what is Christian is not identical with what is of the world. The natural is not identical with the supernatural or the revelational with the rational."[9]

So, although Bonhoeffer demanded a realistic appraisal of the contemporary situation and sought for new ways to present the claims of Christ to his generation, he was not a student of the "God is dead" school.

Writer Ved Mehta reminds us that Bonhoeffer was robbed of life at 39—"before he had been able to achieve his full powers, remaining therefore a shadowy figure who could just be glimpsed in his many books, which considered together presented a man groping with ideas, profound but disturbing and half-born, and showed a person hedged about with contradictions, such as those to be found in *Letters and Papers from Prison*."[10] Bonhoeffer's theological reflections "bear the marks of intellectual isolation and of the abnormal conditions in Nazi Germany during the Second World War."[11]

In numerous ways, the "God is dead" theologians show their disagreement with Bonhoeffer. Van Buren, for example, writes that he would like to solve the problem of secularism "with the help of a method far removed from Bonhoeffer's thought," through linguistic analysis. William Hamilton admits, "We really don't know what Bonhoeffer meant by religion, and our modern study of the problem of religionlessness must be carried on quite independent of the task, probably fruitless, of establishing just what Bonhoeffer meant."[12]

In *Homo Religiosus and Historical Faith,* Hamilton writes that Christians, according to Bonhoeffer, should not regret that *homo religiosus* has died, i.e., that man no longer "needs religion," but that this situation should be accepted so Christian faith can be restated intelligently to a nonreligious generation. "The disappearance of the gods desired by the human mind for its own purposes has opened the way for faith in the one true God," in Bonhoeffer's view.[13] This does not lead to the proclamation that "God is dead."

John C. Bennett, president of Union Theological Seminary, adds: "The great theologian Dietrich Bonhoeffer, who provided stimulus for this frank rejection of the presence of God, would himself have been horrified by the use now made of a few paragraphs in his writings....He believed passionately that God as revealed in Christ was at the center of the world of men who had come of age."[14]

Paul Tillich

Life magazine indicated that the "God is dead" theologians felt a great debt to Paul Tillich, the German existential theologian who taught in U.S. seminaries for many years preceding his death in 1965. In reporting Tillich's death, the Nov. 5 issue of *Life* described a visit between Altizer and Tillich and noted: "Altizer assured Tillich that he, more than any other modern theologian, had 'opened the confrontation with the real world. You fathered us, here we are.' "*

But Altizer expresses regret that both Tillich and Rudolf Bultmann are "closed to Nietzsche's proclamation of the death of God."[15] Actually, for Tillich, atheism and the concept that

---

*The kinship can be glimpsed in some of Tillich's writings: "In classical theology God is, first of all, Being as such." He adds "If today you say that God is Being, it sounds almost blasphemous." (*The Protestant Era*) Nevertheless, Tillich speaks of God in terms of being: "the ground of being," the "abyss of being," or "being-itself."

Since anxiety assertedly belongs to the very structure of being, anxiety is also inevitable in God. This anxiety is due to nonbeing, which is the "depth of the divine." God himself is threatened by nonbeing. According to Tillich, being has ontological priority over nonbeing, but nonbeing is the dynamic first principle. The demonic is the depth of the divine, but never becomes destructive because it is overcome by the resistance of being.

In Tillich's view, ultimate nonbeing is God, God in his depth of Godhead, so that to face this God means that man faces the threat of nonbeing. Man's existential anxiety—about death, futility—is rooted in the God who is nonbeing in his ultimate depth. This reduction of theology to anthropology allows endless vagaries.

"God is dead" is impossible. He attempted a religious interpretation of the world. Instead of a "religionless Christianity," Tillich proposes a definition of religion as being "unconditionally concerned," regardless of whether this concern expresses itself in secular or religious forms. It is assumed that every man has something which he takes seriously and without reservation, that every man has therefore an ultimate concern, and that, in this sense, he is "religious."

In the light of such a definition atheism becomes impossible. Tillich writes: "The paradox got hold of me that he who seriously denies God, affirms Him. . . . There is, I soon realized, no place *beside* the divine, there is no possible atheism, there is no wall between the religious and the nonreligious. The holy embraces both itself and the secular. Being religious is being unconditionally concerned. . ."[16]

Tillich defined God as "the Ground of our very being." He equates God with "depth" or "ultimate concern," i.e. that which is taken seriously and without reservation. Although Tillich's "ground of being" is too ethereal and subjective to satisfy orthodox Christianity, his position cannot be equated with the cry "God is dead."

John A. T. Robinson

If any one man prepared the way for the introduction of the "God is dead" gospel to an amazed public, it probably was Bishop John A. T. Robinson, Anglican Bishop of Woolwich in England. His book *Honest to God* became a bestseller among religious titles in England and America, and millions of people read with astonishment as the respected clergyman questioned the doctrines and viewpoints of the orthodox Christian faith.

Some readers interpreted the bishop's reflections as honest searching for truth, but many others saw it as a sword-in-sheath revolution. The Rev. Nicholas Stacy, rector of Woolwich for three years, evaluated the theological revolution thus:

"While the movement has undoubtedly brought hope and encouragement to many thoughtful people who had dismissed the orthodox faith as incredible, it has also disturbed faithful churchmen who claim to have had their fundamental beliefs undermined. The theological revolution has thrown open a lot of windows. One has to admit that so far more has gone out than has come in."[17]

The radicalness of Robinson's theology is suggested by his close relationship with Episcopalian Bishop James A. Pike of the United States. In a magazine article that featured Pike's repudiation of the doctrines of the triune God, the resurrection of Christ and Christ's virgin birth, Pike was described as on his way to Cambridge University and talks with Bishop Robinson so that he might discover a "faith for the space age."[18]

Bishop Robinson in *Honest to God* wrote: "I have never really doubted the fundamental truth of the Christian faith—though I have constantly found myself questioning its expression."[19] It seems evident that more is actually at stake.

Robinson, questioning the concept of a God "up there" or "out there," concludes that the concept of "height" should be replaced by "depth," thus moving in the direction of Tillich. "This simple substitution can make much religious language suddenly appear more relevant," he declares. "For we are familiar today with depth psychology, and with the idea that ultimate truth is deep or profound."[20]

Although Bishop Robinson recognizes that the word "depth" is equally as symbolic as "height," he nevertheless believes that it may speak more profoundly to the soul of modern man.[21] In his book Robinson manages to achieve a bizarre merger of Bonhoeffer's " 'beyond' in our midst" with Tillich's "ground of all being."

Yet, Robinson's views do not satisfy Hamilton who protests: "Robinson is far too confident about the possibility of God."[22] Even Robinson's nonobjectified theism is rejected by the "God is dead" theologian.

Theologian David Jenkins of Oxford University raises questions regarding the views of Robinson. "Is the 'ultimate reality' of Tillich and Robinson any more objective than the traditional God they reject? Or, alternatively, is the experience of 'ultimate reality' more self-evident and objective than the awareness of the traditional God? And aren't Tillich and Robinson guilty of some legerdemain when, in their eagerness to prevent 'ultimate reality' from becoming simply a subjective experience, they claim for it a sort of objective status and then surreptitiously endow it with personal attributes?"[23]

Robinson speaks of the Christian who is open to the divine *agape* of the universe, and contends that the biblical worldview "grounds all reality ultimately in personal freedom—Love."[24] He also writes: "We are united to the source, sustainer and goal of our life in a relationship whose only analogy is that of *I and Thou*...we are rooted and grounded wholly in love."[25] But if reality at the deepest level is *personal love,* it is perilous logic indeed to disassociate genuine life from a *personal God!*

Although Robinson and Tillich do not line up with the "God is dead" theologians, their influence undoubtedly encouraged the movement. The denial of the objective reality of the God who has revealed himself to man is a long step toward the far-out position that "God is dead."

Harvey Cox

Harvey Cox, of Harvard Divinity School, has contributed to the ferment in radical theology by his portrayal of religionless living in his book *The Secular City*. Secularization has steam-rollered civilization, declares Cox. He describes secularization as "the loosing of the world from religious and quasi-religious understandings of itself, the dispelling of all closed worldviews, the breaking of all supernatural myths and sacred symbols."[26]

When it comes to the question whether God exists or not, Cox feels that it is a desperately serious issue. He says the word "God" emerges from a particular sociocultural setting and that it has virtually become a useless term in our day.

It is quite true that words tend to lose their original power by daily use, and particularly so since the coming of mass communication. The constant barrage of words produces a lowering of the original level. It is probably futile to try to rescue language from this degeneration. Words have suffered by daily use and abuse, and banalization has become characteristic of language. At the same time, the question remains, how can we replace the word "God?"

Cox suggests: "It is too early to say for sure, but it may well be that our English word *God* will have to die, corroborating in some measure Nietzsche's apocalyptic judgment that 'God is dead.' "[27] At the same time he raises the question: "By what name shall we call the one we met both in the life of Jesus and in our present history as the liberator and the hidden one?"

He offers no definite solution, atlhough "presumably God will continue to live eons after English and all other present languages have been totally forgotten. It is only word magic to believe that there is some integral connection between God and any particular linguistic vocable...perhaps for a while we shall have to do without a name for God."[28]

At the same time, Cox is convinced that "God is not simply a different way of talking about man. God is not man, and man can only be really *'responseable'* when he *responds.* One must be responsible *for* something *before* someone. Man, in order to be free and responsible, which means to be *man,* must answer to that which is not man."[29]

Cox says it is both pointless and patronizing for Tillich to suggest to nonatheists that they are really Christians who do not know any better, that the problem is just semantic or conceptual. The absence of God experienced by Cox is similar to the experience of no-god-at-all, but he contradicts Van Buren and contends that urban-secular man does experience transcendent values.[30]

1. Bonhoeffer, Dietrich, *Letters and Papers from Prison,* trans. by Reginald H. Fuller (New York: The Macmillan Co.), 1962, pp. 195-200, 162-169.
2. *Ibid.,* pp. 164-165.
3. *Ibid.,* p. 165.
4. *Ibid.,* pp. 165-166.
5. *Ibid.,* p. 226.
6. *Ibid.,* p. 220.
7. Bonhoeffer, Dietrich, *Ethics,* trans. by Nelville H. Smith (New York: The Macmilan Co.), 1965, p. 121.
8. *Letters and Papers from Prison, op. cit.,* p. 224.
9. *Ethics, op. cit.,* p. 199.

10. Mehta, Ved, "The New Theologian," *The New Yorker*, Vol. XLI, No. 41, November 27, 1965, p. 63.
11. "The New Theologians," *op. cit.*, p. 73.
12. *Radical Theology and the Death of God, op. cit.*, p. 39.
13. Hamilton, Kenneth, "Homo Religiosus and Historical Faith," *New Theology No. 3, op.* cit., p. 54.
14. Bennett, John C., "In Defense of God," *Look*, April 19, 1966, p. 70.
15. *Radical Theology and the Death of God, op. cit.*, p. 109.
16. Tillich, Paul, *The Protestant Era* (Chicago; The University of Chicago Press)', 1963, p. XI.
17. "The Decline of the Church in England," Nicholas Stacey, *Harper's* magazine, March 1966.
18. "An American Bishop's Search for a Space-Age God," *Look* magazine, Feb. 22, 1966.
19. Robinson, John A. T., *Honest to God* (Philadelphia: The Westminster Press), 1963, p. 27.
20. *Ibid.*, p. 45.
21. *Ibid.*, p. 132.
22. *Radical Theology and the Death of God, op. cit.*, p. 24.
23. "The New Theologian," *op. cit.*, p. 100.
24. *Honest to God, op. cit.*, p. 130.
25. *Ibid.*, p. 131.
26. Cox, Harvey, *The Secular City* (New York: The Macmillan Co.), 1965.
27. *Ibid.*, p. 265.
28. *Ibid.*, pp. 266-267.
29. *Ibid.*, p. 259.
30. *Ibid.*, pp. 260-261.

chapter 4

Jesus Christ and the "Blik"

If "God is dead" and "God is Jesus," one might expect very little attention from the radical theologians to Jesus Christ. Actually much consideration is given to Christ, causing theologian Daniel Day Williams to comment wryly: "There is no God, and Jesus Christ is his only-begotten Son." Just what is the role of Christ in radical theology?

Altizer talks about Christ, although he repudiates Christ's resurrection. He wrote in a letter: "When we say that God is dead, we are in fact intending to make a Christian affirmation that God has died in his transcendant form and is now fully incarnate in every human hand and face. It is a way of saying that Christ lives more fully and more comprehensively now than he has ever lived before."[1] The letter was signed: "Yours in Christ, Thomas J. J. Altizer."

Elsewhere, the Christian atheist elaborates: "The true Jesus has passed through his death from a particular to a universal form, and continues to be present in a forward-moving and transfiguring Word."[2] The radical Christian, Altizer points out, does not believe in the "possibility of returning to either the word or the person of the original Jesus of Nazareth. Consequently, the radical Christian rejects both the literal and the historical interpretation of the Bible, demanding instead a pneumatic or spiritual understanding of the word."[3]

The essential, according to Altizer, is the "contemporary presence of Christ." God has ceased to be present in history,

36

but Christ will be with us to the coming of the end of the world. He is present in his word and that word is a word reconciling the world *to itself!*

Altizer says that the word becomes fully incarnate in the concrete actuality of human flesh; it is present wherever that which has been becomes new, or wherever the present seeks fulfillment in a redemptive future. The Christ who lies upon our horizon is the Christ of faith in an eschatological word, and therefore he cannot be fully present in the dark and hidden crevices of a turbulent present, nor can he be fully at hand in the broken body of a suffering humanity.[4]

Apparently we meet Christ to some extent in suffering humanity, but the incarnation is a process moving forward toward a redemptive end. The radical Christian is open to this eschatological end, and maintains this openness by constantly negating all past expressions of the "word." The eschatological word breaks from the future into the present, and by our opening ourselves to the "immediate actuality of the moment before us" we can know Jesus, the one who is present in the fulness of time. The totally incarnate word can only be the Jesus who is incarnate in "every human hand and face." The God who is Jesus appears wherever there is energy and life.

Altizer voices sharp disagreement with most other theologians, stating that the radical Christian has judged theology to be closed to original thinking or imaginative vision.[5]

In his early writings William Hamilton wrote that radical Christians come through Jesus because the god they found apart from him is a kind of absentee enemy who does not make it possible to think or to live as the Christians they wish to be.[6]

Jesus Christ is best understood, says Hamilton, as "neither the object nor the ground of faith, neither as a person, event or community, but simply as a place to be, a standpoint. That place is, of course, alongside the neighbor, being for him. This may be the meaning of Jesus' true humanity and it may even be the meaning of his divinity, and thus of divinity itself."[7]

Hamilton insists that the New Testament record is extremely reticent in ascribing supernaturalness to Jesus and that Jesus was very hesitant about accepting traditional titles such as Christ, Son of God and Son of Man.

A reader of the New Testament can only wonder if Hamilton has read the Book!

For Hamilton, the neighbor is the "bearer of the worldly Jesus," and our way to our neighbor is mapped out by Christ as well as by social, psychological and literary disciplines. The essence of Hamilton's Christology seems to be to find Jesus in one's neighbor. Jesus is reduced to a standpoint, or, as Van Buren might put it, he gives rise to a "blik."[8]

The "blik" plays a significant role in the analysis by Van Buren. A blik involves a perspective and entails a commitment. It is a particular way of looking at the world, a purely subjective attitude. A blik is a frame of reference and principle of interpretation. One cannot speak of a blik in terms of truth or falsehood, but rather in terms of significance or meaninglessness. Some people are optimists and others are pessimists—it is a matter of blik. The Marxist has a blik and so does the Buddhist; both believe they are in possession of a discernment which commits them to certain actions.

The case is the same for the Christian, according to Van Buren. Jesus has become the occasion for a new discernment, a blik, which demands a commitment. The Christian has gained a new perspective and this blik is noncognitive.

Ninian Smart has countered Van Buren: "If Christianity becomes thus noncognitive, it becomes ineffective; for a man cannot rest his life on seeing elephants in the clouds. We can look on the clouds that way: they may look like elephants on a stormy afternoon. But we cannot expect the elephants to descend and to haul logs for us."[9]

Undoubtedly few people would relish the idea that their religion is merely a blik, neither true nor false! They would ask how a blik should be chosen! Why not follow the Marxist line, or become a Muslim? And why deny concrete historical events? Christianity is embedded in history, and the life and resurrection of Jesus Christ did not take place in a corner.

Van Buren had to use the blik concept to give some consistency to his attitude toward history. For he presupposes
that God has not acted in history, that the rise and fall of
empires, the history of the church and missionary endeavor
have moved along without God and therefore without ultimate
goal or purpose.

Van Buren defines history as "an answering of questions
about human action in the past. The answers are found by
means of interpretation of evidence, and they are sought for
the sake of human self-knowledge."[10] His stress on "human" is
strong.

If God is not active in history, he is obviously not active
today, and all of history is ultimately meaningless. As one's
life is interwoven in history, how can it gain meaning? To
speak of meaning in history, declares Van Buren, is to speak
of "the insight and commitment which has arisen out of or is
reinforced by one's reflection upon history. To say that there
is no meaning in history is to say that in reading or hearing
history, no *new* perspective has arisen which might lead to a
commitment."[11]

This makes it clear that the blik is noncognitive, a highly
subjective viewpoint without objective basis. One person's
blik may completely contradict another's, but they are equally
valid, as far as is known. Yet Van Buren indicates that the
Christian faith has some historical foundation after all. He
writes:

"If historians could establish, to suppose an extreme case,
that Jesus had made an agreement with the authorities to
spend his remaining days in the wilderness in silence and let
some other person be crucified in his place, thereby revealing
that he was as insecure and self-interested as his enemies,
Christian faith as the New Testament presents it would be untenable. It would have lost its historical foundation. For this
reason, then, we may take the other side and say that Christian
faith *is* based on history."[12]

Seemingly there must be some objective reality after all

to the Christian faith. The blik could be true or false, after all. If, for instance, Jesus had actually retired into the wilderness and had been replaced by someone else, even this "Christ" might have become the occasion of a blik or new insight for someone. Yet he would have developed a blik based on something "untenable." Van Buren somehow concludes that the historical Jesus is indispensable for faith.[13]

Since all we know about the historical Jesus is contained in the New Testament; at least a partial historicity of the documents is admitted. The question then arises: Who will determine—and what criterion should be used to determine —what is historical in the New Testament and what is "mythological?" This may not be important to Van Buren since meaning for him is only a personal, highly variable response to life.[14]

Van Buren's central affirmation of Christianity is the Easter story, the resurrection of Christ. Whereas Altizer finds a basis for the death of God in the incarnation, Van Buren looks to Easter for the focal point. Not that Easter is a fact— at least not in the ordinary sense of the word. Nevertheless, "something happened."[15] It is crucial to determine what happened, as Easter sets Jesus apart from all other men.[16]

Scripture says that the risen Savior "appeared." Van Buren claims that we cannot verify such a statement by common sense or empirical means. Peter's statement, "He appeared to me," cannot be checked, of course, against empirical data open to any and every competent investigator who cares to examine them.

Van Buren suggests that the way to verify the statements regarding the resurrection is to see if the word and actions of the speaker conform to the statements. The test should be one on consistency.

By way of illustration he cites Hamlet, who claims to have seen his father's ghost and to have been informed by the ghost that his father was murdered. The fact that Hamlet determines to avenge his father's death is strong support of his claim to have seen a ghost.

But if this principle of Van Buren's is accepted, do not the apostles' actions prove that they had actually seen the risen Lord? The center of the apostolic proclamation was precisely the resurrection of Jesus Christ. The despondency of the disciples yielded to courage and their silence to proclamation! Vigorous practical activity resulted from the appearances of the Lord. That the apostolic proclamation did "not intend to assert a physical resuscitation of the dead Jesus," as Van Buren claims, is an extraordinary misreading of the text.[17]

Van Buren says the disciples used words about Jesus Christ which belong to the realm of the "end and goal of all existence, but do not refer to any *thing*"—they simply meant to convey that they "suddenly saw Jesus in a new and unexpected way."[18]

This happened on Easter. The disciples discovered that day the freedom of Jesus was contagious, says Van Buren. But with the word "contagious," charges Langdon Gilkey, we have "jumped back into the murky, unempirical depths of theological, meaninglessness illusions."[19]

Although the extraordinary freedom of Jesus cannot be substantiated, according to Van Buren, the disciples did gain a special insight, a blik, and became aware of the fact that Jesus had been a very free man and that this freedom was contagious. They "caught" the freedom of Jesus, not by choice, but as something which happened to them. Somehow they could not simply tell the story of Jesus as the story of a remarkably free man who had died; the story had to include the event of Easter, the resurrection.

This imaginative interpretation of the resurrection raises more questions and creates more problems than it resolves. Philosopher Karl Jaspers points out that the resurrection "was just as implausible to the contemporaries of Jesus as it is to modern man. To exaggerate the spiritual differences between one age and another," says Jaspers, "leads to overlooking the identical elements that characterize man as such. Thus, materialism and a naturalistic realism have always been with us;

similiarly, man's disposition to believe in the absurd is as unchanged as ever, no less strong today than it was then. . . . The absurd faiths of the modern era, ranging from astrology to theosophy, and from National Socialism to Bolshevism, suggest that superstition has no less power over the human mind today than it had formerly. Such permanent elements of human nature are universal and have nothing to do with modern science, no more than with similarly permanent elements of rationality."[20]

We may ask why was it exactly three days after the crucifixion that the disciples received (from whom?) their new blik? And since the initial discovery was not enough and many doubted, why were appearances granted to the same group more than once? Was it common for a blik to dawn on many people *simultaneously*. . . and perhaps to as many as 500 persons who, according to the record, saw the risen Savior?

Why would the disciples proclaim the *resurrection* of Christ, instead of clearly indicating that they meant something like "freedom?" Why was the blik communicated by the disciples in such equivocal language that most people interpreted the event as an actual resurrection?

The word "resurrection" was not a common theme for the Jews of the day. Martin Buber assures us that the Pharisaic Jew of the day believed in a general or final resurrection of the dead, but: "Resurrection of an individual in the course of history was unknown to him from Scripture. . . and he could not in general make himself believe it."[21] If the resurrection of an individual in the course of history was highly unbelievable to the average Jew, and just as incredible to the average Greek, why would reasonable men use such bizarre and uncontemporary terminology, acceptable neither to Jew nor Greek?

And why allow the misunderstanding to persist? In Athens the Apostle Paul proclaimed the resurrection. The witnesses repeatedly referred to an empty tomb. . . what did they mean if not a bodily resurrection? Why did the disciples persist in communicating their blik in a fashion that fomented threats and endangered their lives? Why did they not explain their proclamation and save their lives?

The Jewish people might well have accepted an innocuous blik and tolerated one more school of thought among them. They would have welcomed an alternative to Paul's dogmatic assertions that Jesus Christ was raised for man's justification.

Would it not be more intelligent and honest to deny the text outright, than to force such a radical reinterpretation of it?

It is strange, too, that this new insight "happened" to the apostles and not to all the people who had known Jesus. Does this indicate that an attitude of openness regarding Jesus Christ was necessary in order to accept the event?

It would seem that Van Buren has banished God in favor of Christ and then banished Christ in favor of his disciples. He reasons in a circle by saying: "You can register how striking and amazing a man Jesus was by his effect on his disciples," and, "The effect on the disciples has to be taken seriously... because it was a reaction to such an extraordinary man."[22]

The ascribing of deity to Jesus Christ, says Van Buren, sprang from the new freedom on Easter which was somehow derived from Jesus Christ. "He set men free," says Van Buren, and it seemed to the disciples "that they had stumbled on a great truth [sic], which was true before they came to see it. It was in this sense 'objective.' The decisive event was one which they felt had happened to them, and which alone made it possible for them to 'decide.' "[23]

Suddenly "truth" is pried into the picture, an objective truth, existing before the disciples grasped it! They stumbled on it (or did it happen to them, contagiously?). An event took place—not a resurrection— but a new perspective, and choice became possible. Actually the "event" was the new perspective, the blik, and the "event" was the choice...a choice not altogether free since contagion made it almost inescapable that it would "happen" to them!

Van Buren concedes that the Christian, because of his

blik, will be liable to use "final words" in speaking of Jesus, words of awe, of wonder and of worship. Even the language of praise and adoration is appropriate, says Van Buren, such as "God of God" and "light of light," "very God of very God." Of course, such words merely inform the hearer of the new insight which has been gained and commend to him an attitude.

Van Buren is not yet done with the Easter event and its blik. He states that there is no possibility of demonstrating that Jesus was freer than any other man. Historical evidence about Jesus is not established; the Gospel accounts are not entirely trustworthy; therefore we know little about the historical Jesus.

There is, it would seem, no overpowering reason to prefer Jesus to any other person with characteristics of greatness. Albert Camus could "yield" such a blik to some readers, and the same holds true of Socrates and numerous other persons.

Van Buren holds the position that "God is Christ" and writes: "Since there is no 'Father' to be found apart from him, and since his 'Father' can only be found in him, the New Testament (and this passage specifically) gives its answer to the question about 'God' by pointing to the man Jesus."[24]

The New Testament passage referred to is John 14:9 and 10: "Jesus said to him [Philip], 'Have I been with you so long, and yet you do not know me, Philip? He who has seen me has seen the Father; how can you say, 'Show us the Father?' Do you not believe that I am in the Father and the Father in me? The words that I say to you I do not speak on my own authority: but the Father who dwells in me does his works.'"

The assimilation of all theology to Christology is a most serious error. Even in this passage Jesus speaks of the Father as a distinct person and states: "No one comes to the Father, but by me...the Father dwells in me." The fact of the union is indisputable on the authority of Christ; the mode is inexplicable, but some of the results are indicated in the words "the Father...does his works." (John 7:16-18) The Father is revealed in the life of the incarnate Son. The unity between Father and Son is indissoluble and Christ does not hesitate to call attention to the self-evident quality of his works.

The simple identification of God with Jesus undertaken by Van Buren represents a serious deviation from the traditional faith of the Christian Church—a deviation sometimes called a 'unitarianism' of the Second Person. Asserts Macquarrie: "For while Christian faith has maintained that 'Christ is God,' this has never been regarded as a convertible proposition, that is to say, we cannot turn it around and say 'God is Christ.' "[25] The Christian God, the God who reveals himself in the Bible, is Father, Son, and Holy Spirit.

The biblical claim that Christ is not an assertion of identity, but a predication of Christ's Godhead. Even a superficial reading of the Gospel will compel one to admit that Jesus believed that he was sent and that he obeyed "someone" whom he called "Father."

At this point Van Buren can only conclude that "the Gospel of John, as well as the logic of language, forces us to silence before all questions concerning that 'one.' "[26] It would seem that logic moves the other way since the Gospel of John—of all Gospels—makes it crystal clear that Jesus is the Son of God, and the logic of language leads to the inevitable conclusion that the Gospel was written that "you may believe that Jesus is the Christ, the Son of God." (John 20:30)

"In a sense," wrote a *Time* magazine editor, "no Christian doctrine of God is possible without Jesus, since the suffering Redeemer of Calvary is the only certain glimpse of the divine that churches have. But a Christ-centered theology that skirts the question of God raises more questions than it answers. Does it not run the risk of slipping into a variety of ethical humanism? And if Jesus is not clearly related in some way to God, why is he a better focus of faith than Buddha, Socrates or even Albert Camus?"[27] These incisive questions must be answered by those who hold the view that "God is dead."

It is obvious that the life of Christ was lived on the premise of God the Father. The first recorded sentence of Jesus and that which was probably his last both contain a reference to his "Father." In each of the five prayers where the words of Jesus are given, he addresses God as "Father." He deliberately avoided the abstractions used in the synagogues and in vogue at the time, such as place, etc.

God, who is the Father of all men by virtue of creation, allows his sun to shine on all; God, who is love, cares for all men. This message was at the heart of Christ's proclamation. There is no such thing as preaching Christ unless we also proclaim that he mediates the knowledge of God and the salvation of God.

1. Correspondence with Norman Vincent Peale, *Christian Herald,* May 1966, p. 37.
2. *The Gospel of Christian Atheism, op. cit.,* p. 56.
3. *Ibid.,* p. 25.
4. "Word and History," *op. cit.*
5. *The Gospel of Christian Atheism, op. cit.,* p. 77.
6. *The New Essence of Christianity, op. cit.,* p. 72.
7. *Radical Theology and the Death of God, op. cit.,* p. 92.
8. At one point Hamilton wrote, "I believe that the resurrection of Jesus can be affirmed as an ordinary event; the empty tomb tradition, at least, seems to me to contain historical material of a high degree of probability.... The resurrection means the making present and available to men of faith the form of Jesus' Lordship as a form of humiliation and suffering." *The New Essence of Christianity, op. cit.,* p. 116.
9. "The Intellectual Crisis of British Christianity," *New Theology No. 3, op. cit.,* p. 22.
10. *The Secular Meaning of the Gospel, op. cit.,* p. 110.
11. *Ibid.,* p. 114.
12. *Ibid.,* p. 126.
13. *Ibid.*
14. *Ibid.,* as developed in the "blik" concept.
15. *Ibid.,* p. 128.
16. *Ibid.,* p. 164.
17. *Ibid.,* p. 130.
18. *Ibid.,* p. 131.
19. Gilkey, Langdon, "A New Linguistic Madness," *Journal of Religion,* Vol. XLIV, July, 1964, pp. 238-243.
20. *Myth and Christianity, op. cit.,* p. 5.
21. Buber, Martin, *Two Types of Faith* (New York: Harper & Row), 1961, p. 100.
22. "The New Theologian," *op. cit.,* p. 138.
23. *The Secular Meaning of the Gospel,* op. cit., p. 170.
24. *Ibid.,* p. 147.
25. "How Can We Think of God?" *op. cit.,* p. 45.
26. *The Secular Meaning of the Gospel, op. cit.,* p. 148.
27. "Toward a Hidden God," *op. cit.,* p. 85.

chapter 5

Radical Christianity in Action

It is apparent that the "God is dead" theologians, though few in number and perhaps limited to three, are not in agreement among themselves. Altizer proclaims the self-annihilation of God in the incarnation and subsequent death of Jesus, since God is Jesus. Van Buren also holds the view that God is Jesus, but refuses to say anything about the God worshiped by Jesus. Hamilton views himself as a man waiting for God in unbelief.

As to Jesus Christ, Van Buren sees the centrality of the resurrection "happening," but denying the actual event he takes refuge in a subjective "blik." Altizer finds Christ in every human hand and face, whereas Hamilton finds in Jesus Christ a standpoint. What, then, is the message of the "radical Christians?" Altizer sums it up in the slogan: " 'No' to God and 'Yes' to the moment before us." Theology is no longer informed by the will of God, but by the world[1]

It must be difficult to propose a definition of faith which would go hand-in-hand with a theory that "God is dead." For Altizer, faith is 'The mediation between faith and history." Van Buren says faith consists in acknowledging that a liberation has taken place; Jesus of Nazareth reveals what it means to be man. For Hamilton faith is a place, a being-alongside one's neighbor, and ethics is summed up in love for one's neighbor.

What happens to love for God? It is equated with love for the neighbor by Van Buren.[2] The command to love God first *and* the neighbor can only mean, he says, that we are to love the neighbor on the model of Jesus and in his freedom. If this is all the text can mean, why retain the idea of "love for God" at all? The answer is not given.

Hamilton also believes that to find Jesus in the neighbor is the sum and substance of Christian ethics. But this love is not secure nor confident. It is not *agape*, but more like *eros* or passion.[3] The devotion of the Christian must be given to the *polis*, i.e., the city, politics, the neighbor. The "city" is defined in terms of power, culture, art, sex, money, the Jew, the Negro, beauty, ugliness, poverty and indifference. Therefore the Christian movement should be characterized by a worldliness that with the abolishing of the transcendent the source of guilt and judgment has disappeared and the total union of God (!) and man is now possible—a union actualizing a new totality of love. Love to God, the foundation of these actions in orthodox Christianity, is ignored.

At the end of Van Buren's book *The Secular Meaning of the Gospel,* he attempts to reinterpret some cardinal Christian doctrines such as creation, providence, prayer. Speaking of prayer, Van Buren reminds us that ancient man prayed for rain on his neighbor's field, thinking that he was doing the most effective thing possible. By his prayers he hoped to be of help to his neighbor.

Today the "profane Christian," with the same motivation, would study the situation and perhaps suggest irrigation. If no solution to the problem is possible, he will at least stand by his neighbor and help him through hard times. This is the new meaning of intercessory prayer as defined by Van Buren. It simply means to "hold the situation up to God" or what one might call "reflection." The radical Christian studies the problem and endeavors to be of help. If this is impossible, at least he will have "exercised himself in the intensity of thought" which is demanded by the Christian blik."[4]

Is there any advantage, then, in being a "Christian atheist" rather than a "Buddhist atheist" or a "Hindu atheist?" Van Buren assures us: "The fact remains that the history of Jesus is not the same as the history of Buddha." Further, he says that the one who has received his freedom from Jesus would not agree that all sources of freedom are the same. At the same time he declares that Jesus' uniqueness cannot be demonstrated, that in reality little is known of the historical Jesus, and that we know next to nothing of the freedom of Jesus.

How can the Christian choice be justified? Christian faith demands a "minimal acquaintance with the Gospel narratives," Van Buren claims,[5] yet he states elsewhere that all free men, even though they never heard of Jesus, received their freedom from the one and only source Jesus.[6]

Van Buren labels his reinterpretation of doctrine as a "reduction in the content of theology." He compares the process with "the sort of reduction which has been made by modern culture in many fields," for instance: "Astrology has been 'reduced' to astronomy" and alchemy to chemistry![7]

Altizer's alterations are more sweeping. He says that all Christian morality may have to be sacrificed. He questions the possibility of moral judgment, for forms of such judgment may be barriers to the realization of energy and life. Moral law is an alien power, he alleges, and guilt and resentment are crutches.

It is obvious that every moral imperative addressed from a beyond perishes for the man who believes that God is dead. Such a man may risk moral chaos and his own damnation, Altizer concedes. He frankly warns:

"The contemporary Christian who bets that God is dead must do so with a full realization that he may very well be embracing a life-destroying nihilism; or, worse yet, he may simply be submitting to the darker currents of history, passively allowing himself to be victim of an all too human horror."[8]

Thus the willing of the death of God may be a way to madness, and even to the most totalitarian form of society in history.

For our part, we believe that Dostoyevsky was right: If God is dead, all is permitted. If all Christian morality is subject to change, presumably even love to the neighbor—so highly praised by Van Buren and Hamilton—then Sartre's dictum that "hell is other people" can be valid. For a person to risk damnation, to bet that God is dead, to live without moral imperatives, to gamble that the death of God leads to liberation and not to nihilism, to sanity and not to madness, reflects an unholy defiance and personal pride which the Bible calls rebellion that will fall under the judgment of God.

It is basically irrational for men who advocate such radical views to maintain that they are "Christians,"—profane, contemporary, secular—but "Christians." It would have been more coherent, respectable and honest to advocate an unadorned atheism or pantheism, unfettered by references to Christ and the New Testament. Why not confess to radical atheism, or moderate atheism, rather than speaking of a "Christian atheism" which is linguistic nonsense.*

Hamilton clings to his claim on Christianity. He believes that the New Testament Jesus "can in fact be known" and can be a figure of sufficient clarity to be a possible center for Christian faith and discipleship. His personal faith as a "Christian atheist" might be summarized in his statements: "Attention to Jesus does this for me"; and "The time of the death of God is also the time of obedience to Jesus."

Since all we really know about Jesus is found in the pages of the New Testament, does this mean that Hamilton recognizes the historicity of at least some pages of the Gospels, though he feels that the Bible is a strange book which does

---

*Christian atheism has little appeal to authentic atheists. "Stated another way, if they [atheists] were to be attracted to Jesus Christ and Christian claims, they would prefer to confront something of the sometimes embarrassing and often inspiring context and tradition in which they have appeared and have been affirmed. They [atheists] averred that they preferred a more misfit, angular type—the spiritual people who seem to be related to a spiritual depth not easily accessible outside the tradition—to those who seem to opt for facile accommodationism, who want to be immediately relevant to the secularists but who still want to talk about Jesus and the servant church." "The Turn from Mere Anarchy," Martin Marty and Dean Peerman, *New Theology*, No. 3.

not come alive except for a psalm, a prophetic call, a piece of Job, perhaps some words of Jesus?[9] Is this "attention to Jesus" or "obedience to Jesus"?

Hamilton defines a Christian as a man "obedient to him [i.e. Jesus Christ] and obedient as he was obedient." Jesus demanded obedience to his commandments and he said, "Believe in God, believe also in me." Can a declaration of the death of Jesus' Father be obedience to Jesus?

Jesus made clear to whom he was obedient: "My food is to do the will of him who sent me, and to accomplish his work. . . . I have come down from heaven not to do my own will, but the will of him who sent me." Does it make sense, Oriental or Occidental, to proclaim the death of God, the one whom Jesus said he was obeying, and at the same time to claim obedience to Jesus?

Jesus spoke with extraordinary authority, and the reaction of the crowd is related in all four Gospels: "The crowds were astonished at his teaching for he taught as one who had authority. . .they were astonished at his teaching, for he taught them as one who had authority, and not as the scribes. . .his word was with authority. . .no man ever spoke like this man. (Matt. 7:28, 29; Mark 1:22; Luke 4:32 and John 7:46)

At one point Jesus was interrogated as to the source of his authority and he answered by telling the parable of a man who planted a vineyard. He rented it out to some farmers and went away to a distant land. When harvest time came he sent one of his servants to collect his share of the crops. The tenants beat him up and sent him back empty-handed. Then he sent another servant, but the same thing happened. Finally he sent his cherished son, and the tenants killed him (Luke 20).

The context of the parable establishes that Jesus' authority was unique because he was the unique Son of the eternal Father. Obedience is indeed due to Jesus, precisely because he is the Son! If God is dead, Jesus is not the Son of God, his claim to authority is empty and no obedience is due him. The best that could be said of such a schizophrenic personality would be that he was a mad genius.

If a profane mode of existence is chosen, if all transcendence has been swallowed up in immanence, if man has chosen absolute autonomy and abolished every notion of the sacred, how can one sanely claim "Christianity?"

Altizer insists. In comparing the virtues of oriental mysticism with Christianity, Altizer chooses the superiority of Christianity, saying that oriental mysticism is a "backward movement," a movement back to the primordial Totality, a process of involution, whereas Christianity is a forward-moving process, directed to the future, to the End. The uniqueness of Christianity, says Altizer, is not the central person, Jesus Christ—as maintained by Van Buren and Hamilton—but evolving truth as discovered in the forward-flowing incarnation.

Nietzsche considered the death of God to be dreadful news, and consistently carried his nihilism to its inevitable conclusion. His thinking, says Karl Jaspers, "seems an expression of everything corrosive in the modern age. If we follow Nietzsche to the end, nothing remains of existing ideals, values, truths, realities."[10]

If it is true that "God is dead," albeit by Altizer's mode of self-annihilation, the highest values are void, purpose vanishes, nihilism remains. Nothing binds the individual, nothing holds —no law, no value, no norm. Everything is meaningless, and man is the victim of some cosmic catastrophe, flung into an alien universe.

1. *The Gospel of Christian Atheism, op. cit.,* p. 10.
2. *The Secular Meaning of the Gospel, op. cit.,* p. 183.
3. *Radical Theology and the Death of God, op. cit.,* p. 93.
4. *The Secular Meaning of the Gospel, op. cit.,* pp. 188, 189.
5. *Ibid.,* p. 144.
6. *Ibid.,* p. 142.
7. *Ibid.,* p. 198.
8. *The Gospel of Christian Atheism, op. cit.,* pp. 127, 146.
9. *Radical Theology and the Death of God, op. cit.,* p. 90.
10. Jaspers, Karl, *Nietzsche and Christianity,* trans. by E. B. Ashton, (U.S.A.: Henry Regnery Co.), 1963, p. 97.

chapter 6

Man In Crisis

We are told by the radical theologians that we live in a post-Christian era, that the Christian world has collapsed and we traverse an age of crisis. Throughout the Western world, they say, a decisive shift is taking place which may be the biggest since the Protestant Reformation, and there is no longer need or place for God in our world. What is this crisis of which they speak?

Science is one cause of the crisis. John Macquarrie explains it this way: "With the rise of modern science, with its increasing and apparently unlimited capacity for accounting for events within the world in terms of other events within the world, the need for positing such a God has gradually been eliminated."[1]

Though scientific concepts do dominate our culture, must this inevitably lead to the theological conclusion that "God is dead?" Is there complete antagonism between science and supernatural Christianity?

Science does not provide a total worldview, nor even attempt to furnish one. Science is conscious of its own limitations and the particularities of its insights. Science explores beings in the world, not Being itself. Science leaves the ultimate questions untouched: Where does the world come from? Where is it going? What is the supreme value? What is the meaning of life?

The radical theologians claim that Christianity is divisive and oppressive and must therefore be abandoned. Would a scientific worldview from which God is excluded be less oppressive and absolute? Not in Karl Jaspers' judgment. He writes:

"An alleged knowledge of what we are, or can be, or want to be, or alledgedly cannot help being, begets a new intellectual intolerance, presenting as universal truth that which is valid only for the thinker's own life, on the grounds that it is modern, of the age. The tendency of many rebels to absolutize their own rootlessness in nothingness originates in that false idea, not in any scientific advance by a scientific philosophy."[2]

Theologian George A. Buttrick exposes the fallibility and subjectivity in science. "Our sciences, by their very method, reflect our present purposes which are to fulfill rational and extend possessive control...[science is] a prisoner of its own framework, the study of a fraction of the world [the natural order] by a fraction of the mind [the radical and analytical mind]."[3]

Nicholai Berdyaev sees science as a restricted discipline. He writes: "Science is man's reaction for self-preservation; man, lost in the dark forest of the world's life. In order to live and develop, man must consciously orient himself in the given world which crowds upon him from every side. For this protective orientation man must bring himself into correspondence with the realities of the world.... Science is a highly perfected means of adaptation to the given world and to the necessity forced upon us.... Science is not creativity but obedience; its element is not freedom but necessity." Similarly: "Culture comes from necessity rather than freedom, from adaptation rather than creativeness." (*Meaning of the Creative Act*)

Protests against an exaggerated status for science preceded the modern age. The novelist Dostoyevsky mocked the utopian "crystal palace" presented at a scientific exhibit in London. He scoffed at the time when "new economic relations will arise, relations ready made and calculated in advance with mathematical precision, so that all possible questions instantaneously disappear because they receive all the possible answers."

Dostoyevsky raises the question: What joy will man derive from functioning like a timetable?[4] Gabriel Marcel declares that the term "timetable" already describes many lives, and deplores the moment when the individual is reduced to an agglomeration of functions.[5]

It is frequently assumed that theology starts off with many unprovable presuppositions whereas no such weakness exists in scientific investigations. Actually, all knowledge involves presuppositions, whether in the realm of science or theology.

The experience of most persons is rather limited, so that most information is received via testimony, the report of reliable witnesses. This is true for all study of history, for instance, but also for most scientific data since few people can be "experts" in more than one scientific discipline. To test the reliability of the witnesses, to assure that they are free of bias, to be confident that the information which is transmitted is correctly understood, all of this is usually assumed and theories are built on the information received, although not substantiated by personal experience.

Experience obviously is not the sole source of knowledge, or else it would be impossible to explain the exceptional certainty which is conceded to mathematics. Nor can the acceptance of "necessity" be derived from experience alone, because even the widest experience supplies us with only a limited number of cases; all our experiences never tell us what happens in *all cases,* and consequently does not yield incontrovertible truth. In addition, experience always involves an element of faith, of instinctive confidence in the reality of that which we experience. It is difficult enough to demonstrate the reality of our own existence, let alone the reality of the world around us. If nothing is assumed, by scientist or theologian, nothing can be established.

Science always assumes the existence of a fixed, stable order. Only if the world is a *cosmos,* not a *chaos,* can it be investigated and become intelligible. It is assumed that behind the changing features of the world is a fixed, stable order, and cognition is the ascertainment to discover the *being* of things. It is consistent to assume that this being has a quality akin to our natural intellect.

Science is an interpretation of facts. Facts alone do not give us reality; they might even obscure it. The Greeks used the word *aletheia* for truth, which means to uncover, to remove the veil which hides things. Science observes, tests and verifies facts of the physical universe.

Science becomes a work of imagination as well as observation when it develops a construction, a model. Science moves from observation to classification and bases "laws" on them, then applies these laws to additional observations. This procedure presupposes the constancy of the phenomena, the uniformity of nature, the capacity of rational thought, and an orderly universe as the object of observation.

A few optimists have traditionally held that science leads to moral wisdom, but their faith is regularly tested both by human events and their own colleagues. That there is no necessary correlation between scientific progress and human happiness,—no direct ratio of growth between secularity and contentment,—is recognized by many scientists, among them the Nobel Prize physicist Max Born.[6]

It should not be overlooked that, regardless of all else, the scientific observer must possess certain ethical qualities. Openness, honesty, persistence and initiative are necessary qualities to "receive" truth in scientific pursuits as well as in moral or religious.

Nietzsche maintained that Christianity produced the will to absolute truthfulness, and this moral force acted as a goad to promote the concept of universal science, the endeavor to know the full truth about the world, man and history.

Christians engaged in scientific disciplines would strongly controvert the viewpoint that modern science demonstrates that "God is dead." The fantastic accomplishments of modern science are awesome, but the operative principles in "modern" science are not recent discoveries.

According to Karl Jaspers, modern science proper began in the late Middle Ages, although its realization dates only from the 18th century.[7, 8] William Hamilton speaks of the scientific revolution which occurred in the 17th century.[9] It is unreasonable to derive radical metaphysical conclusions from the principles of "modern" science which have been operative for centuries. It does not appear that scientific men are flocking to the banner of the "God is dead" theologians because of any compatibility of such a proclamation with the latest scientific insight.

Another cause of the crisis is said to be the secularization of man's culture, creating an insuperable obstacle to any Godward-aspirations.

Secularization—to be distinguished from secularism—has been defined as a process "in which society and culture are delivered from tutelage to religious control and closed metaphysical worldviews."[10]

To the secular man, life is a set of problems, not a deep mystery. He wastes little time thinking about "religious" questions and lives with highly provisional solutions.

John Killinger, of Vanderbilt University, defines secularism as "the final effects of the desacralization process, by which in turn we mean the transference of culture from a base in the holy to a base in the profane."[11]

But for many people, secularism is a concealed *religious* attitude. Vahanian admits that for them "the present and the immanent are invested with the attributes of the eternal and the transcendent."[12]

Even "modern man" is religious, and if he is attached to the outward, the transitory and the unreal, he invests this "love of the world" with "religiosity." That religion plays a significant role in the life of "secular man," that it is very much a part of the "ground rules" needs no formal demonstration. Such groping need not be inauthentic for being rudimentary, and it would seem that secular, modern man has an "ultimate concern" after all.

Christian teaching has had a significant impact on Western culture in past centuries, but it is questionable whether this culture was truly "rooted in the holy." In any case, if secularization has rooted contemporary culture in the profane, this does not invalidate historic Christianity, for it flourished in precisely such an atmosphere. The early church faced a culture anchored in the profane—or, worse, in the "religious," which was a greater obstacle to the proclamation of the one, holy God.

In spite of his commitment to linguistic analysis, Van Buren fails to give a precise definition of the word *secular* which plays a key role in his book, *The Secular Meaning of the Gospel.* Secularism, he says, is a "loose designation of the reaction to the Idealism of the last century."[13]

According to the dictionary, "Idealism" maintains that the "real" is of the nature of thought; or that it describes the tendency to represent things in an ideal form, as they might be rather than as they are, with emphasis on values. Secularism, then, would be a description of things not as they might be, but as they really are.

Van Buren demands that the word "real" be interpreted in harmony with certain "ground rules' which exclude the concept of God, because such an idea is not valid for modern man.[14] He feels that anyone adhering to the Christian Gospel faces a basic choice: Being a Christian is something "religious and quite distinct from secular affairs, or Christian faith is a human posture conceiveable for a man who is part of secular culture."[15] In other words, the Christian must either choose to be "religious," which is equated with being out of touch with the world of secular affairs and reality, or he must decide to be "secular" which means to be out of touch with historic Christianity.

Such a basic choice is only necessary if the secular is equated with the real and God is eliminated from the "ground rules." In the past it has never been a problem to be "religious," i.e., to live a God-centered life, and at the same time to be active in the world.

The Christian participates actively in the affairs of the world. Is it necessary to recall political movements such as Christian Socialism, or the influence of Christianity on the arts and sciences? It is acknowledged that slavery was abolished in England through the energetic action of a "small pressure group composed mainly of evangelical Christians, who proceeded to organize a relentless campaign against the British slave traders, and later, with equal success, against the institution of slavery in Britain's overseas territories."[16] Many Christians today feel that Christian commitment demands involvement in the realm of politics, the arts, economics, and science.

The question remains: Who defines "modern man," and who represents him? Could Sartre and his atheism function in this capacity? Bultmann no less than Van Buren assumes that he speaks for modern man, yet Van Buren is highly critical of Bultmann.[17]

Does "modern" mean final, definitive, and if so does it imply that tomorrow will be similar in all essentials to today? Does "modern" mean that from now on progress merely advances along a road identical to the one already under our feet? Has all history been preparation and aspiration toward the present moment, the modern man? Or does not every generation look upon itself as the culmination of the past? Modernity is not a criterion in itself, and cannot be appropriated by the radical theologians. (Appendix A).

The voice of a historian should be heard in regard to "modernity" and the past. In *The Rise of the West,* the University of Chicago's William McNeill writes: "The 'disruption' that became palpable in the first part of the twentieth century was not a disruption at all but simply a further stage of its own inner evolution...

"Throughout history, drastic instability has distinguished the Far West from the other great civilizations of Eurasia; and one may view the recent history of the world as yet another instance of this long-standing proclivity for revolutionary reorganization, in which not solely Westerners but all mankind has this time been entangled...

59

"The heirs of other cultural traditions generally prefer the view that 'modern' civilization differs from all older styles of life in more important respects than it resembles any one of them. Agreement under these circumstances cannot be expected; and men of the twentieth century obviously lack the time perspective needed for an emotionally neutral and perspicacious assessment...

"Even the very best observers of the twentieth century may well turn out to be as limited in their insight into the world around them as the cultivated Greco-Romans of the first century A.D. who remained entirely insensitive to the future importance of the tiny Christian communities of their time. But these are limits inherent in the human condition, which we necessarily share with our heirs and successors as well as with former generations."[18]

If, then, we are under the impression that we live in a time of extreme crisis and that great upheavals are characteristic of our day, we should not overlook the estimate of a historian. As he says: "The cultural coherence of distant epochs may be partly illusory. Much variety and confusion is simply lost and forgotten, for, to survive at all, art and thought must always be filtered through meshes imposed by the tastes of later generations."[19]

"...Lengthening time perspectives often reduce the irreconciliabilities of an age to facets of a larger unity, much as the view from a high-flying plane, by blurring details, can turn the intricacies of a landscape into a map. Some centuries hence, therefore, the main lines of artistic and intellectual development of the 19th and 20th centuries may appear as straightforward as those of any other epoch."[20]

The same author comments on the secularization of opinion which took place in Europe as the 18th century advanced, and which was simultaneously transforming the U.S., even affecting Puritan Massachusetts. In this same 18th century religious conformity was no longer mandatory in many European states, and individuals were permitted to follow their own religious inclinations.

The note of desperation, so prominent in the 16th century struggles for theological and metaphysical certainty, died rapidly after the Thirty Years' War. The demand for orthodoxy in word, thought and deed diminished. The intellectual leaders began to concentrate their attention on science and rationalistic philosophy rather than on theology.[21]

The Newtonian revolution played a significant role. Isaac Newton himself was a committed Christian, but people concluded from his scientific theories that God, architect and master mathematician of the universe, could most effectively manifest his wisdom and the excellence of creation by retiring from active supervision of the "machine" he had called into being. Intervention would supposedly demonstrate the inadequacy of God's established laws. Little room was provided for divine grace or providence. In the Newtonian universe it was just as difficult to find a suitable "geographic location" for heaven and hell as it is today.

It would seem, then, that the "modern" cry is not so modern after all. Ortega y Gasset says: "Properly speaking, technology in the fullness of its maturity begins around 1600, when man in the course of his theoretical thinking about the world comes to regard it as a machine."[22] The Newtonian universe seemed to leave little room for a personal God and led some to proclaim deism.

Christianity survived this crisis, and history would suggest we have reason to believe that Christianity will survive the present crisis—if indeed we live in a state of crisis.

At one time Paul Tillich undertook to analyze his "situation" and assumed that he stood at a crucial moment of history, a *kairos,* a moment rich in content and significance. He expected the coming of a new, theonomous age, open and directed toward the divine. He became the leader of the Kairos circle in Berlin and participated in the religious-socialist movement shortly after World War I. Tillich lived long enough and was humble enough to admit that his analysis was incorrect and that history took another path. The belief that transitions cannot be made without catastrophies had to be abandoned.[23]

Does the announcement of present crisis by a few contemporary theologians carry a greater guarantee of exactitude than Tillich's? After World War I the mood was highly optimistic; it seemed that a new beginning was dawning. After World War II the mood was pessimistic; a "mood of the end" prevailed, with the "clock" of the atomic scientists pointing close to historical "midnight." Could not the second reaction be as mistaken as the first?

Back in 1860 Pierre Joseph Proudhon wrote in one of his letters: "Today civilization is in the grip of a crisis for which one can only find a single analogy in history—that is the crisis which brought the coming of Christianity...All traditions are worn out, all the creeds abolished; but the new program is not yet *ready,* by which I mean that it has not yet entered the consciousness of the masses. Hence what I call the dissolution. This is the cruelest moment in the life of societies...decay, and decay for a period whose end I cannot fix and which will last for not less than one or two generations —is our lot...I shall witness the evil only; I shall die in the midst of the darkness."[24]

But listen to Ortega y Gasset: "The greatest crisis through which the European destiny has ever passed ends with Galileo and Descartes—a crisis which began at the end of the 14th century and did not taper off until the early years of the 17th century. The figure of Galileo appears at the end of this crisis like a peak between two ages, like a divide that parts the waters. With him modern man enters into the modern age."

What is called "crisis" is, in historical perspective, no more than a transition which man makes from his attachment to and reliance on one set of things to embracing and depending on another set of things. History has been defined as the science of transition. Even in decadent or crisis periods some things germinate whereas others decay. There are positive elements in every era which demand thoughtful evaluation.

Perhaps a consciousness of crisis is characteristic of each generation, at least to some extent. Even if the "crisis concept" should gain acceptance in our era, we should remember that other days of serious crisis—the barbarian invasion of the Roman Empire, the earth-shaking announcement of Galileo, the Newtonian Revolution—these did not necessitate the acceptance of any such radical view as "God is dead."

1. "How Can We Think of God," *New Theology No. 3, op. cit.,* p. 42, 43.
2. *Myth and Christianity, op. cit.,* p. 10.
3. Buttrick, George A., *Christ and History,* (New York, Abingdon Press), 1963, p. 31.
4. MacAndrew, Andrew R., *Notes From Underground,* (New York, New American Library) A Signet Classic, 1961.
5. Marcel, Gabriel, *Philosophy of Existentialism,* Translated by Manya Harari, (New York: The Citadel Press), 1964, pp. 11, 12.
6. "Though I love science I have the feeling that it is so much against history and tradition that it cannot be absorbed by our civilization. The political and military horrors and the complete breakdown of ethics which I have witnessed during my life may be not a symptom of an ephemeral social weakness but a necessary consequence of the rise of science—which in itself is one of the highest intellectual achievements of man. If this is so, there will be an end to man as a free, responsible being. Should the race not be extinguished by a nuclear war it will degenerate into a flock of stupid, dumb creatures under the tyranny of dictators who rule them with the help of machines and electronic computers."
"The Reflections of Max Born," *Bulletin of the Atomic Scientists,* Nov. 1965.
7. Jaspers, Karl, *Nietzsche and Christianity,* (U.S.A.: The Henry Regnery Company), 1961, pp. 74-75.
8. *Myth and Christianity, op. cit.,* p. 5.
9. *Radical Theology and the Death of God, op. cit.,* p. 47.
10. *The Secular City, op. cit.,* p. 20.
11. "The Uses of Agnosticism: Secularism in Modern Literature," *The New Theology No. 3, op. cit.,* p. 133.
12. *Death of God, op. cit.,* p. 67.
13. *The Secular Meaning of the Gospel, op. cit.,* Preface XIII.
14. *Ibid.,* p. 83.
15. *Ibid.,* p. 17.
16. Oliver, Roland and Page, J. D., *A Short History of Africa,* (Baltimore: Penguin Books), p. 136, cf. 165.
17. *The Secular Meaning of the Gospel, op. cit.,* p. 68.
18. McNeill, William H., *The Rise of the West,* (Chicago: University of Chicago Press), 1964, pp. 15, 728, 729.
19. *Ibid.,* p. 753.
20. *Ibid.*
21. *Ibid.,* p. 669, 683.
22. Gassett, Jose Ortega y, *History As a System,* New York: W. W. Norton and Company), 1962, p. 117.
23. *The Protestant Era, op. cit.,* pp. 59, 60.
24. Buber, Martin, *Paths in Utopia* (Boston: Beacon Press), 1960, p. 34.

chapter 7

A Relevant Faith

According to the radical theologians, the development of the modern city has destroyed the concept of a living God. The words of Harvey Cox in *The Secular City* are typical:

"The rise of urban civilization and the collapse of traditional religion are the two main hallmarks of our era, and are closely related movements." He adds: "No correlation is more definite or more constant than that between a given economic level of society and the nature of the supernatural beings postulated by the tribe at large or by the religious individual in particular...When man changes his tools and his techniques, his ways of producing and distributing the goods of life, he also changes his gods."[1]

Supposedly, then, the invention of the wheel, the ability to ride horses skillfully into warfare (900 B.C.), the introduction of the traction plow (some time before 3000 B.C.), the invention of the battle-ax and the light, two-wheeled war chariot (1700 B.C.)—these technologies of battle and means of livelihood which transformed the social balance of Eurasia should have profoundly affected the religious picture of those days, but no information to that effect is available!

It is true, of course, that the city has become central to the destiny of modern man. It is also true that modern man thinks, feels and responds distinctively in the city. Metropolitan man is subjected to an unusual volume of stimulation, and learns to react against his environment in order to protect himself and keep his sanity. He learns to preserve at least some of his individuality in the face of strong social forces. The gravitation toward isolation and anonymity of the modern city-dweller has been dramatized skillfully by Franz Kafka, whose heroes are reduced to Mr. K., the unknown citizen who is measured in terms of statistics.

Despite these forces, the institutional strength of the Christian church in the United States is at an all-time high. Public faith in God seems as secure as it was in medieval France. According to a 1965 survey by Pollster Lou Harris, 97 percent of the American people say they believe in God. In 1964 church membership rose by 2 percent, compared with a population gain of about 1.5 percent. More than 120 million Americans claim a religious affiliation. A recent survey indicates that 44 percent of them attend church services weekly.[2]

Yet, if urban man is suffering a loss of identity, is not a greater sense of personality needed? Is not personality the mark of high development? Personality underlies thinking, feeling and willing. It is expressed in terms of motivation, purpose and love. Must God be depersonalized because society is depersonalizing man, and are we once more fashioning a god in our contemporary image?

If the city dweller's mind is crowded with impressions that eliminate time for reflection, if he develops a craving for novelty and is characterized by impatience, then we might recognize that this is nothing new under the sun. For the Apostle Paul met people in Athens who spent their time in telling or hearing something new. Paul proclaimed the living God to this urbane society and demanded personal repentance. The Christian church originated in the metropolitan centers of the Roman Empire and beyond the Empire, and spread from these centers of civilization and culture to remote rural areas.

It is only arrogance and ignorance to suppose that men of a previous age were less perceptive and intelligent than in our era. To consider the Gospel significant for ancient metropolitan centers and inadequate for the modern megalopolis is supercilious. It is as misguided as Bonhoeffer's observation has proved to be: "The age of big cities on our continent seems to have come to an end."[3]

Why increasing urbanization should require the abandonment of a personal God is as mysterious as the premise that modern technology and emperical science necessitate the conclusion that "God is dead."

It is obvious that "urban man" and his worldview predominate only in the Western world, and more particularly to the United States where technology and urbanization have made great strides. Is it necessary, then, for the whole world to conclude that "God is dead?" Is this the new proclamation of Christian missions?

William Hamilton writes that the group of men who announce the death of God have "a strong sense of being in a particular place, urban America, and at a particular time; born in the twenties...very conscious of being white."[4] Are we offered a concept which is devoid of universal validity and cannot be meaningful to areas where cultural patterns are different? Should yet a different gospel be proclaimed to rural America and people living in Africa, Asia and other parts of the world? How can such a variable "message" be equated with the Gospel of Christ, the good news addressed to all men as universally valid and eternally true?

Is God not still alive for the rest of the world? Are they still deluded? The mission of radical theology would then be to bring its liberating message of the death of God to peoples throughout the world—from the jungles and the primitive areas to the most sophisticated and established cultures!

The presuppositions of the "God is dead" theologians are precarious, parochial, and highly subjective. Their weaknesses cannot be concealed behind esoteric, dogmatic affirmations. Such statements as "The greatest theological problem of our time is an understanding of the meaning of the death of God" will not be accepted by thinking Christians, urban or rural.

Those who advocate the death of God desire to be relevant to contemporary man. This, indeed, may be the ultimate motivation of the movement. By discarding an ancient world picture and adopting a "modern outlook" they hope to capture the imagination and attention of disoriented people.

But what if Gabriel Vahanian's judgment is correct? He said, "Modern man is neither awed by the death of God nor perplexed by the problem of suicide. He is represented neither by Nietzsche nor by Camus."[5] In that case, modern man does not probe nor despair. For him, the message "God is dead" would be another case of too little, too late, and the "good news" of God's death would be ignored in a post-Christian era where no one cares.

And why should the radical message be meaningful to the avowed atheist? For God to be meaningfully dead, he had to have once been meaningfully alive. But this was never the experience of atheists. For them, the traditional God was not there in the first place and so could not disappear or die. There is no room in their lives for anguish or the anxiety of doubt—rather at the most a mild curiosity. The atheist does not need God, because he has "found himself" and is content with his achievements and prospects.

The Apostle Paul, preacher and missionary, did not listen to the world to receive a message for the world. In Athens he did not hesitate to quote Greek poets, and in Antioch, speaking to Jews, he reviewed Jewish history and indicated its culmination in Christ. He became "all things to all men"—without losing sight of man's essential need for reconciliation with God through Christ. Therefore he always proclaimed *salvation,* with due regard for the cultural environment.

The radical Christian does not believe in the possibility of maintaining either the word or the person of the historical Jesus of Nazareth. Revelation is not seen as a disclosure of God in Christ or in propositional truths, but as a forward-moving process from the primordial Being of God to the god who becomes all in all in the End.

Is this message of the Christian atheists relevant to our pragmatic age? Does this mystical view parallel the technological development of our times?

The desire to be relevant is laudable, but radical theology goes beyond that, as the *Christian Century* sardonically commented: "The point is for the seminary to become so pertinent to modern culture that it has nothing to say to that culture." Religion should not only have the word that others have; the preacher should not only echo the language of the daily newspaper and radio; true religion will not simply follow the general trend or be content to accept public opinion as normative.[6]

It is important to be relevant—but it is essential to have the true message, a message with power to change men for the better. The Christian message should not merely inspire enthusiasm, give reassurance or bestow dignity. The proclamation must convey spiritual strength and lift above human enthusiasm, certainties and dignities. In the light of the Word everything human must be transformed, judged and transcended. The Christian proclamation does far more than consecrate a given situation.

The true Word of God, we're told, is sharper than the sharpest dagger, cutting swift and deep into innermost thoughts and desires with all their parts, illuminating us as we really are. (Hebrews 4:12)

Vahanian, in spite of his general pessimism, seems to see some relevance in contemporary Christianity: "In the field of arts, too, religion has in the last decade made a comeback, the importance of which far exceeds the spectacular publicity of the revival of the '50s."[7] Literature is still "God-haunted" as college students read Camus, Hemingway, and T. S. Eliot.[8] Saul Bellow is one of several "God-haunted" authors who made the best-seller list.

Tillich and Buber have not lost all relevance; religious debate is of deep interest on the campus; Billy Graham attracts large crowds, especially young people, and thinks that we may have America's most religious-minded generation of youth.[9] It is vastly exaggerated and premature to say that "modern man" has made the choice to live a profane mode of existence.

Man does not live by bread alone, said Jesus, but by every word that proceeds from the mouth of God. Humanity's deepest problems cannot be met by the world. Forgiveness of sins and eradication of guilt, the inspiration of true love, can only come from God the Creator. Many persons are not conscious of their deep needs and have learned to live with provisional solutions, absorbed in the temporal, material and ephemeral. Such a "love of the world" is possible, but if anyone so loves the world, says the Bible, love for the Father is not in him.

Bonhoeffer reacted against a *mechanical use* of God to solve some human problem, but at the same time it is clear that a dependent relationship to God is the Christian position.

We must not overlook that Christ did call to man in his needs: Come unto Me if you hunger, thirst, desire life, look for rest, seek healing. The Bible instructs us to delight in God and enjoy Him—and the distinction between enjoyment and abuse of God goes back to Augustine. Man does *need* God. The individual cannot even be truly human by himself.

As Berdyaev put it: "Man can only be interpreted through his relation to God."[10]

1. *The Secular City, op. cit.*, p. 1
2. "Toward a Hidden God," *Time*, Vol. 87, No. 14, April 8, 1966, p. 82.
3. *Letters and Papers From Prison, op. cit.*, p. 182.
4. *Radical Theology and The Death of God, op. cit.*, p. 182.
5. *The Death of God, op. cit.*, p. 132.
6. Nielsen, Charles M., "The Loneliness of Protestantism," *Christian Century*, September 15, 1965, pp. 1120, 1121.
7. *The Death of God, op. cit.*, p. 82.
8. "Student Market Examined at NACS Annual Meeting," *Publishers Weekly*, May 16, 1966, pp. 35, 36, 37, 38.
9. Graham, Billy, "God Is Not Dead," *U.S. News and World Report*, April 25, 1966, pp. 74-82.
10. Berdyaev, Nicolas, *The Destiny of Man*, (New York: Harper and Row), 1960, p. 46.

chapter 8

Good News or Bad?

The Christian Gospel is preeminently "good news"—the divine initiative in bringing salvation to the human predicament. The Word of God takes a realistic view of man, presenting him as the apex of God's creation, reflecting the divine image, but living in misery and a sense of estrangement, having cut himself off from God by willful rebellion. Yet redemption remains possible, and God's love initiates it. Man can be transformed and reflect once again the image of God.

The greatness of man is evidenced in his recognition of his misery. A stunted tree does not know itself to be miserable. In this sense all the miseries of man prove his essential greatness. Man is not miserable without feeling it. Pascal at this point brilliantly exegetes the Scriptures. This view of man is sane, balanced.

The existentialist who denies God has a thoroughly somber view of man. The lines of Sartre in *No Exit* are well-known: Hell is...other people. Man is a contradictory being, an unhappy consciousness. To be man is to try to be God, and yet this unquenchable thirst to be God is futile. Man is a useless passion. According to existentialists, *angst*, anxiety, is at the core of man's being. The isolation of man, the alienation of man, the absurdity of the human situation—these themes are found so frequently in the existentialists that they dominate all else.

From a literary angle, William Golding writes the *Lord of the Flies* to illustrate the depravity of man. Even Bishop Robinson condemns the naturalistic view of man because of its shallowness in estimating what is wrong with the world.[1] Tillich speaks of the estrangement from the origin and aim of life and feels that something radical, total, unconditioned is demanded of man. Sartre views man as a victim of some cosmic catastrophy, flung into an alien universe to which he is bound by nothing. Both theologians and existential atheists who deny a personal God describe the despair of man and paint a dark picture of the human condition.

Strangely, while philosophers without God find existence a dead-end, the radical theologians display confidence. Somehow the "death of God" has produced a joyful ecstasy. The autonomy of man, freedom from repression and restraint, these are the dominant notes of the glad tidings that "God is dead." *Angst,* despair, futility, alienation, isolation, nihilism, all are allegedly overcome by the magic words: "God is dead." Sartre is often quoted, but the pessimistic conclusion he reaches from the premise of the non-existence of God is rejected.

Altizer enlists Sartre's support and ignores him in turn. One point where Altizer finds help is Sartre's mysticism. He writes: "Sartre has provided a mystical theology for the atheistic mystic, and...his most basic ontological categories are derived from the death of God."[2]

It is highly significant, however, that *Sartre's atheism preceded, not followed, his philosophical investigations.* In his autobiographical book, *The Words,* Sartre says he was "led to disbelief not by the conflict of dogmas, but my grandparents' indifference." He relates a childhood experience, describing how at one time he had a feeling that God existed.

"I had been playing with matches and burned a small rug. I was in the process of covering up my crime when suddenly God saw me. I felt his gaze inside my head, my hands. I whirled about in the bathroom, horribly visible, a live target. Indignation saved me. I flew into a rage against so crude an indiscretion, I blasphemed, I muttered like my grand-

71

father: 'God damn-it, God damn-it.' He never looked at me again."

Sartre describes another incident in 1917 when he was only 12. It happened in La Rochelle, where young Sartre was waiting for some schoolmates with whom he was to go to the Lycee.

"They were late. After a while, not knowing what else to do to occupy my mind, I decided to think of the Almighty. Immediately he tumbled into the blue and disappeared without giving any explanation. 'He doesn't exist,' I said to myself with polite surprise, and I thought that the matter was settled. In a way, it was, since never have I had the slightest temptation to bring him back to life."[3]

It appeared to Sartre that the autonomy of man could only be achieved if the death of God was recognized! Therefore, it is "wise" and "necessary" to recognize it. Fact is irrelevant, all is subjective. Sartre objected to the "look of God," feeling his gaze. At this point he echoed Nietzsche who proclaimed that God *had* to die because: "He saw with eyes that saw everything; he saw man's depths and ultimate grounds, all his concealed disgrace and ugliness...He always saw me: on such a witness I wanted to have revenge or not live myself. The god who saw everything, *even man*—this god had to die! Man cannot bear it that such a witness should live."[4]

The case against God was thus built by Sartre and Nietzsche on their own desires and fears! Facts were a secondary consideration.

Though Sartre and Nietzsche both concluded that "God is dead," their reactions to this "good news" differed. Altizer chooses Nietzsche's response, declaring that the "historic event" of the death of God has created an ecstatic liberation, an ecstasy felt by Nietzsche, Rilke and Proust as they were freed from the supervision of an omnipresent God.[5]

Hamilton sees a move from pessimism to optimism in three areas: the social sciences, the field of art, and the civil rights movement. He cites the movie *A Hard Day's Night*—a Beatles' first, no less—and even the famous Beatles' sound as samples of this new mood of celebration and rejoicing.*

Bonhoeffer, from whom Hamilton claims to draw some inspiration, had quite a different viewpoint. He spoke of the disunion of God with man and said that for such a man all things are in disunion, what is and what should be, life and law, knowledge and action, idea and reality, reason and instinct, duty and inclination, conviction and advantage, necessity and freedom, exertion and genius, the universal and the concrete, the individual and the collective.

Presumably, all these tensions are now overcome, thanks to the death of God. Picasso, who saw the twentieth century as a time when everything cracks, everything is destroyed and everything isolates itself, and other artists who "see" similar desolation are simply mistaken.

This optimism seems to be based on wishful thinking. It faces despair, not with the conviction that out of it God can bring hope, but with the conviction that the human conditions which created it can be overcome; it faces death, not with the hope for immortality, but with the human confidence that man may befriend death and live with it as a possibility always alongside.[6]

Is the God of Christian theology a tyrant who deserves death? Does he emasculate man, hinder his creativity and limit his responsibility? Are these values restored by those who proclaim the death of God?

Theologian John C. Bennett warns: "The humanity of man can be threatened if the final word is that he is alone, that he is responsible to no authority above the state or the other powers of the world that claim his allegiance. The deepest source of his freedom may still be that he knows that he must 'obey God rather than men'."[7]

Egocentric freedom is subjective arbitrariness. Its splendor is an illusion, for it delivers man up to his drives and instincts, to do in any given moment what caprice and passion dictate.

---

* Beatle John Lennon expressed the view in early 1966 that his group is now "more popular than Jesus." He added: "Christianity will go...it will vanish and shrink....Jesus was all right, but his disciples were thick and ordinary."

To desire such freedom, deficient in purpose and content, is to move toward nonbeing. This freedom *from,* rather than freedom *to,* is a self-centered thralldom which impoverishes and blights the personality.

Genuine freedom is freedom from the constraint of the moment. It is expressed in willing obedience to laws whose validity is freely recognized and accepted. It is, ultimately, submission to the highest law, the law of God which is the law of love.

In the measure that the Christian loves God he is truly free, since love burns up necessity and yields freedom. Man can be enslaved only to that which is alien and hostile to his welfare. What is near and dear is not felt as compelling. Those who know God as a Father, reconciled to mankind, love him because he first displayed his love. Obedience is freely given, because the yoke has become easy and his commandments pleasurable.

Sartre demands freedom and equates it with autonomy. At the same time he frequently uses the expression "condemned to freedom," which seems to indicate that such freedom is a loss, a deprivation. According to Sartre freedom coincides at its roots with the nonbeing which is at the heart of man.

But Jaspers reminds us: "Absolute independence is impossible. In thinking, we are dependent on experience which must be given us, in living we are dependent on others with whom we stand in a relation of mutual aid."[8]

Martin Buber echoes a biblical thought when he writes that the true community arises only through people "taking their stand in living mutual relation with a living Center, and, second, their being in a living mutual relationship with one another."[9]

There are two great commandments in the Christian faith, and the sequence of these commandments must be observed. Love to God is preeminent, and this love precipitates love to fellowmen. Such love generates freedom, releases man from paralyzing fear, and then creativity can have full play.

It is not surprising that mankind's great cultural achievements have been traced back to the Judeo-Christian influence. Numerous historians and philosophers find the roots of modern science in the "Christian" atmosphere. *Creativity* is a natural attribute for the person who reflects the image of God the *Creator!*

The biblical picture of God, the revelation of God manifested in Jesus Christ who is the image of God *par excellence,* portrays a God of love to whom the Christian responds in love, freeing him from fear and guilt so that the highest degree of creativity can be reached by redeemed man. Altizer's presentation of God as the "alien other" is a fanciful caricature, a man-made idol which has nothing in common with the true God except the name!

Perhaps Christian atheism was born out of despair, Ortega y Gasset alleges: "When one despairs of any form of life, the first solution which always occurs, as though by mechanically dialectic impulse of the human mind, the most obvious, the simplest, is to turn all values inside out. If wealth does not give happiness, poverty will; if learning does not solve everything, then true wisdom will lie in ignorance."[10]

We might add, if one dislikes Almighty God, then simply say that he is dead!

1. *Honest to God, op. cit.,* p. 79.
2. *Mircea Eliade and the Dialectic of the Sacred, op. cit.,* p. 131.
3. *The Words, op. cit.,* pp. 63, 64, 157.
4. Kaufmann, Walter, *The Portable Nietzsche,* (New York: Viking Press), 1965, p. 378.
5. *The Gospel of Christian Atheism, op. cit.,* p. 22.
6. *Radical Theology and the Death of God, op. cit.,* p. 169.
7. "In Defense of God," *op. cit.,* p. 70.
8. *Way to Wisdom, op. cit.,* p. 115.
9. *I and Thou, op. cit.,* p. 45.
10. *History as a System, op. cit.,* p. 132.

chapter 9

Waiting for God

The rejoicing of the radical theologians over the "death of God" is curiously mingled with a waiting for his return. Both Altizer and Hamilton speculate on this possibility, but it is not important to them now, and they do not anticipate God's appearance as have some dramatists and novelists.

In Beckett's play *Waiting for Godot,* two tramps, Vladimir and Estragon, are waiting for a mysterious Godot. They are waiting for a future that will redeem a meaningless and empty present. Mr. Godot has not been seen by them; he had been talked to, but the evidence comes from another day and the present witnesses give conflicting testimony regarding the character of Mr. Godot. As a matter of fact, Godot may not be worth waiting for. The second and last act of the tragicomedy ends almost exactly like the first:

Vladimir: Well? Shall we go?
Estragon: Yes, let's go.
            They do not move.[1]

The word *Godot* is probably a combination of the English word *God* and the French diminutive ending *ot.* The play seems to underscore that an existence without faith in something beyond man is futile. Sydney Lamb has said of modern tragedy that it must be concerned with "the death of an old God, and the failure of science and materialism to give any satisfying new one, in which the primitive instinct could find a meaning for life, and comfort in its fear of death."[2]

The atmosphere in *Waiting for Godot* is far removed from the vitality and optimism advocated by Hamilton. Beckett represents the theater of the absurd, with the typical existential themes of futility and isolation. This tragicomedy is not indicative of the presumed move from pessimism to optimism which Hamilton thinks is gaining ground and is made possible by the "death of God."

Traces of God are seen throughout literature. John Killinger deplores the "outcropping of spiritual presence" in contemporary authors. He asserts that "too many are still God-haunted." As examples, he cites D. H. Lawrence, Hemingway, Faulkner and Kafka. He adds: "Robert Lowell and John Updyke and Saul Bellow, each of whom has written a significant volume within the last two years, are not at all abashed to talk about him [God]...they do not find him unfashionable."[3]

In *The Great Wall of China* Kafka introduces a small parable concerning a message sent by the Emperor "to you, the humble subject, the insignificant shadow cowering in the remotest distance before the imperial sun." Unfortunately the messenger sent by the Emperor never reaches the end of the innumerable corridors and chambers. The imperial message is never delivered. Meanwhile, "you sit at your window when evening falls and dream it to yourself."[4]

The "waiting" suggested by Hamilton has more cheerful tones, similar to the ones sounded by Melville in *Moby Dick*, a book frequently cited in the death-of-God literature.

"There are certain queer times and occasions in this strange mixed affair we call life when a man takes this whole universe for a vast practical joke, though the wit thereof he but dimly discerns, and more than suspects that the joke is at nobody's expense but his own. However, nothing dispirits and nothing seems worth while disputing... As for small difficulties and worryings, prospects of sudden disaster, peril of life and limb; all these, and death itself, seem to him only sly, good-natured hits, and jolly punches in the side bestowed by the unseen and unaccountable good joker. That off-sort of wayward mood comes over a man only in some time of extreme tribulation."[5] Melville describes this mood as a "free and easy sort of genial desperado philosophy."

In the Christian perspective, the "Emperor's message" has been delivered: Jesus Christ came into the world and through him the revelation of God has reached man. He is the image of the invisible God and the light of the world, illuminating man. The Psalmist "waits for the Lord, more than watchmen for the morning," but his waiting was different from Hamilton's. The Christian waits with firm expectation and hopes with assurance, unlike the dreaming described by Kafka, the futile waiting dramatized by Beckett and the genial despairing of Melville. If God is dead, waiting is pointless.*

The Christian rejects both the exaggerated pessimism and the unfounded optimism and maintains with the Scripture a realistic view of man, of his nobility and his depravity and his possible re-creation. The present is indeed an oppressive wait for some people—there are times when life appears brutal, trivial or just stupid. But death remains a frightful reality for many who face it, and the message that "God is dead" will hardly be "good news," be the dying man ever so modern and sophisticated.

What determines whether—and how—a person waits for God? Basic convictions, or presuppositions, are the prerequisites of all other convictions. Man functions as an entity, his intellect being related to and influenced by his volition and emotions. Often personal desire and feeling become the "reason" for accepting a given belief, but knowledge sometimes depends on will and feeling; at least, knowledge does not function in isolation. And since will and feeling are in their turn informed by knowledge, it would seem we function in a tight

---

*In *Wait Without Idols* Vahanian writes of Melville's hero: "In his megalomania Ahab imagines, furthermore, that transcendence can result simply from a technical victory over the world, over nature, over Moby Dick—as well as over his own reality. Ahab has, in other terms, reduced existence to *Dasein*, that is, to the dimensions of a difficult but not impossible technical problem, like the skillful pursuit of a whale.

cyclical system. This interdependence easily rejects unwelcome new facts, so that truth may be resisted unless there is an honest openness to evidence.

It is tempting for a person to collect only some of the arguments, to follow inclinations and reject objectivity. Or the arguments may be collected, but a full examination declined. Rejection—or acceptance—may thus be based on superficial grounds, because the new idea is contrary to preconceived notions, to established traditions or the opinions of recognized leaders. The concept may demand a transformation of life or apparently lead to consequences which appear absurd at the time. Perhaps intellectual laziness, indifference, or self-sufficiency discourage thoroughness. Receptivity to truth—for scientist and seeker of God—is a prime factor in recognizing truth.

Christian faith is trust in God and his self-revelation. This revelation depends for its veracity and convincing influence on the moral character of Christ. For this reason the ultimate question of Christianity remains: What do you think of Christ?

The words of Christ are recorded in Scripture. The textual accuracy of these books, the realism and objectivity of the witnesses are confirmed by historical research. For these reasons, faith in the God of the Bible is commanded. (I John 3:32) It is not a "blik" nor a leap into the dark. Faith is not a type of knowledge with a low degree of evidence, supported by religious authority, but a reasonable, genuine response to a reliable, self-revealing personality.

As Ortega y Gasset says, "Each individual before doing anything must decide for himself and at his own risk what he is going to do. This decision is impossible unless one possesses certain convictions regarding the nature of things around one, the nature of other men, or oneself. Only in the light of such convictions can one prefer one act to another, can one, in short, live."[6] For the Christian this decision involves a conviction regarding God.

Man must ever be grounded on some belief, and this belief will shape the structure of his life. The most far-reaching changes in life spring from changes of belief, for they are the ground beneath our feet. It is important to distinguish *Weltbild* and *Weltanschauung*, the world picture and the worldview. The former belongs to the horizontal dimension and is subject to change; the latter belongs to the vertical dimension and is not affected by change in ideology and meaning.

✿   ✿   ✿   ✿   ✿

One day when Jesus was preaching on the shore of Lake Gennesaret, great crowds pressed toward him. He noticed two empty boats at the water's edge and their owners washing their fishnets. Stepping into one of the boats, Jesus asked Simon Peter to take him out a little into the water so that he could sit in the boat and be heard better by the crowd. When he finished speaking, he said to Simon, "Now go out where it is deeper and let down your nets and you will catch a lot of fish!"

The result is described this way in Luke 5:1-8 of *Living Gospels*: " 'Sir,' Simon replied, 'we worked hard all last night and didn't catch a thing! But if you say so, we'll try again.' And this time their nets were so full that they began to tear! A shout for help brought their partners in the other boat, and soon both boats were filled with fish and on the verge of sinking! When Simon Peter realized what had happened, he fell to his knees before Jesus and said, 'Oh, Sir, please leave us, for I'm too much of a sinner for You to be around.' "

The exclamation of Peter reveals the man. His confession of sin was elicited by the spectacle of a miracle of Christ. Peter did not merely express wonder or surprise, but a sense of personal sin.

Wherever Jesus went, his presence produced this sense of sin; even one of the two brigands dying on the cross beside Jesus confessed his sins.

The life of Peter had not been one of crime or gross immorality. He had been a disciple of John the Baptist and lived a life of righteousness, external regularity and inward devotion. But in the presence of Christ he felt the contradiction between the holy and the unholy, the sacred and the profane. Jesus obviously possessed supernatural powers and Peter feared that it was not safe to remain in his presence.

Fear is a normal reaction when man comes face to face with a manifestation of the divine—even when the divine power is used to bless. In the proximity of such power Peter feared inward exposure and possible destruction, and he fervently begged Christ to depart.

All men, like Peter, are conscious of breaking the moral law. How can unpleasant consequences be avoided? God is "alien," say the radical theologians, oppressing, limiting, and threatening man in his freedom, creativity and autonomy. Nietzsche and Sartre sensed God's power and shrank back in fear and hatred, so deeply repelled that they proclaimed the death of God.

Fear always creates distortion. Fear of God generates a caricature of God, distorting his image. Instead of the majesty and glory of God, we see a false god, malevolent, fickle, indifferent, and not nearly as benevolent as ourselves in caring for a mixed-up world.

Fear is a basic element in the relationship of many people with God. Because of fear—of destruction, judgment, calamity —they endeavor to appease God by incantations, rites, magic, self-immolation, self-sacrifice. An incomplete knowledge of the divine attributes contributes to this fear.

God's omnipotence assures that he can strike at any time; his omniscience indicates that nothing is hidden from him; we stand defenseless before God. Is there any refuge or respite? Where can it be ascertained that God is loving and merciful? Creation will not prove it, conscience will not confirm it, reason may not discover it. But Simon Peter found it.

A few years after the spectacular catch of fish, another miracle occurred on the same lake. In the interval, Peter had forsaken fishing to follow Jesus. Then Jesus was crucified and the disciples were shattered. But Jesus rose from the dead, and his disciples awaited his directions.

Once again a few of the apostles had fished all night

81

in vain. Then, in response to a stranger's call from shore, they cast their net on the other side of the boat and the net filled. The reaction produced by this miracle was fundamentally different in Peter. His companion John, the man of instuition, immediately recognized his resurrected Master. Peter, the man of action, leaped into the sea to reach the shore faster. He was anxious to meet the Lord! Why the urge to reach Jesus, whom Peter had once begged to leave him?

Christ, acclaimed by Peter as "the Son of the living God," had died on the cross since the first miraculous catch of fish. Christ's voluntary death assured Peter that "God is love," and that God's love is not dependent upon the reaction of those whom he loves. God loves man regardless of his sin and guilt, and God took the initiative to save man; it was precisely because of the desperate situation of man that Christ came into the world. Now Peter eagerly reaches toward Christ, yearning to be in his holy presence.

This was also the experience of Paul, summarized in Romans 8. He states that "God is for us"—not against us, not indifferent, remote or dead. Here is the quintessence of the good news: *God is for us!* There is only one possible demonstration of this wondrous fact, and Paul describes it: "He did not spare his own Son, but gave him up for us all."

God is not theatening nor oppressive, anonymous nor anemic, defunct nor dead. God is for us. His power, wisdom, justice and all his attributes are operative "for" man, not against him. There is no reason to fear, to stand before him in terror. His power becomes the foundation of life, his wisdom gives direction to life, his immutability guarantees his faithfulness.

The testimony of Paul to this effect in Romans 8 is remarkable. He asserts that nothing can separate us from this divine love, not persecution, nor death—which plays such a large role in existential writings; nor life—with its temptations, seductions, and secularism; not things present—here and now, material, psychological; nor things to come—concern for the future, death; not height nor depth—ups or downs; nothing will ever be able to separate us from the love of God in Christ Jesus our Lord.

This is a note of triumph, of pure optimism based on God, of courage to be, of activity and quiescence, of assurance without presumption. Here is a life lived in the deep consciousness that God is alive and that God is for us. This experience of the true believer is the most positive, the most convincing and the most powerful answer to those who assert that "God is dead."

"God is our strength...we will not fear though the earth should change and though the mountains shake in the heart of the sea....There is a river whose streams make glad the city of God....God is in the midst of her, she shall not be moved ....The nations rage, the kingdoms totter; he utters his voice, the earth melts...the Lord of hosts is with us." (Psalm 46)

1. Beckett, Samuel, *Waiting for Godot* (New York: Grove Press), 1954, p. 60.
2. Lamb, Sidney, *Tragedy* (Toronto: Canadian Broadcasting Corporation), 1965, p. 59.
3. "The Uses of Agnosticism: Secularism in Modern Literature," *New Theology No. 3, op. cit.*, p. 133.
4. Kafka, Franz, *Selected Short Stories of Franz* (New York: Random House), 1952, pp. 129-147.
5. Melville, Herman, *Moby Dick* (New York: The Crowell-Collier Publishing Co.), 1962, p. 242.
6. *Man in Crisis*, W. W. Norton Co., N. Y., N. Y., p. 132.

chapter 10

*"...darkness was upon the face of
the deep...the Spirit of God was
moving over the face of the deep
...God said: Let there be light."*

It is not easy to determine when a decisive shift takes place in history, but it is quite evident that the contemporary era is fundamentally new. In past ages people thought in terms of absolutes. The concepts of true and false, cause and effect were clear and simple. Logic prevailed in its classical forms. The gradual shift may have begun with Hegel. He endeavored to erect a supreme rationalistic system, confident that man could know absolute truth. For him the absolute was a movement, a process, an evolution. Hegel used a dialectical method to build his spiritual monism.

Dialectical logic demands logical contradiction as a necessary stage in the process. For instance, in a series of causes and effects such as A-B-C-D, A would not be a cause unless it effected B, so A owes something to B—it is *because of B* that A is a cause. Therefore, B is not only the effect, but also the cause of the cause of A. Hegel concluded that every effect is the cause of its cause and every cause is the effect of its effect. There is no absolute cause—all is relative. This constant reciprocal action seemed the key to reconcile thesis and antithesis in a supreme monistic synthesis.

Kierkegaard reacted against this extreme rationalism. He

accepted the dialectic process, discerned thesis and antithesis everywhere, but failed to find a rational synthesis. His solution was a leap of faith, irrational but true. If this leap is refused —the rational approach seemingly having failed—the only other alternative would be to abandon all hope, stop seeking a solution and proclaim absurdity...*a la* Camus. Kierkegaard made the leap of faith, and truth for him was inward, personal, particular, paradoxical, subjective and relative.

Gradually these ideas spread. Geographically they moved beyond Germany, culturally they spread from the philosopher to the man on the street (relativity in ethics) and moved from philosophy to the arts (Cezanne and Impressionism) to the sciences (relativity, principle of uncertainty) and finally to theology.

Nietzsche was conscious of these trends and their ultimate conclusions and he proclaimed the death of God (an event not yet known to his contemporaries). Nietzsche influenced Heidegger who in turn exercised a significant influence on Sartre. Vahanian writes: "Existentialism is possible only in a world where God is dead or a luxury, and where Christianity is dead. It originates in the death and decay of Christianity. It presupposes the death of God, although in some of its aspects it may wish that God had not died." (*The Death of God,* p. 227).

Existentialism moves from the objective to the subjective and explores the moods and anxieties of man's inner life. Hence its preoccupation with dread and death. Existentialism moves from the general to the particular, from the abstract to the concrete, and stresses meaning rather than event. For Sartre, existentialism is "nothing but an attempt to draw the full conclusions from a consistently atheistic position." (*Existentialism is a Humanism*) For Sartre, God is dead.

Similarly, Heidegger describes himself as a man who has experienced the death of God, and Jaspers looks for transcendence in the inner self, the depth of man. The silence of God (Sartre), the absence of God (Heidegger), the concealment of God (Jaspers), the hiddenness of God (Bultmann), the eclipse of God (Buber), the nonbeing of God (Tillich) are contemporary expressions of those who in different ways have proclaimed the death of God. With Tillich we have moved from philosophy into theology. And Altizer declared his indebtedness to Tillich.

It is quite evident, then, that the cry "God is dead" is related to the broad contemporary situation. It is the expression of a slow evolution of thought, moving from Hegel to our own day and culminating quite logically in the proclamation that "God is dead." The existentialists offer little choice: nihilism with anxiety and despair, or an optimism rooted in a new mysticism. The prospects of the latter are poor because our era is not given to mysticism. Is nihilism, nothingness, the only choice left?

Or could it be that man in this extremity will once again undertake a total reversal of all values? Could this existential despair be succeeded by a new hope based on the living God? Such total reversals have occurred before. When man has reached the depth of anxiety and despair, he may learn once again to pray with the Psalmist: "Out of the depths I cry to thee, O Lord! Lord, hear my voice....There is forgiveness with thee....I wait for the Lord, my soul waits, and in his word I hope. (Ps. 130)

appendix A

ACCORDING to T. S. Eliot, "No culture has appeared or developed except together with a religion: according to the point of view of the observer, the culture will appear to be the product of the religion, or the religion the product of the culture."[1] If this analysis is correct, no culture can ever be isolated from the religious.

If Western civilization is regarded as "Christian" because it has been influenced by Christian principles, then, according to Eliot, two possible viewpoints should be considered. "The first is that a society has ceased to be Christian when religious practices have been abandoned, when behavior ceases to be regulated by reference to Christian principle, and when in effect prosperity in this world for the individual or the group has become the sole conscious aim. The other point of view, which is less readily apprehended, is that a society has not ceased to be Christian until it has become positively something else."[2]

If, however, Western culture is rooted in the profane, and if this is especially the case for the United States, it is essential to acknowledge this so that the illusion of a "Christian nation" can be shattered. But if the atmosphere is strictly secular, profane, if the motto is forward, not upward, and the outlook horizontal, not vertical, if ambition has replaced aspiration and the spiritual is sacrificed for the material, the Christian Gospel with its demand for transformation is certainly relevant. The proclamation of the death of God in such a situation is only an expression of agreement with the contemporary dilemma—if this dark picture adequately portrays it.

It is exaggerated to state that "the essence of Christianity is embodied in the cultural realizations of the West." Harvey Cox is more correct in stating that the Gospel "is not simply the religious sanctification of Western cultural values."[3] The Gospel is not bound to a particular culture and has been proclaimed in other cultural settings most effectively.

Actually, the Christian church has entertained many different views regarding the relationship of Christianity and culture. The main viewpoints have been summarized by H. Richard Niebuhr in *Christianity and Culture*. He defines culture or civilization as the "total process of human activitiy and the total result of such activity." It is the "artificial, secondary environment" which man superimposes on the natural.[4] The author indicates at least five basic interactions between Christianity and culture:

1. Opposition between Christ and culture, or Christ *against* culture (Tertullian)
2. Agreement between Christ and culture, where Jesus appears as the great hero of human culture history, or the Christ *of* culture (Abelard)
3. Christ as the fulfillment of cultural aspirations, but entering into life from above with gifts which human effort cannot attain, or Christ *above* culture (Aquinas)
4. A dual allegiance is suggested, with man viewed as a citizen of two worlds—Christ *and* culture (Luther)
5. A conversionist solution is proposed; Christ *changes* culture (Augustine, Calvin)

The relationship may be conceived as one of rejection, idealization, synthesis, dualism or transformation, but in no case can culture simply be identified with Christianity so that a new culture rooted in the profane would make Christianity unnecessary and require men to confess that "God is dead."

Nor is the answer found in dichotomy. A clear distinction must be maintained: the Christian is *in* the world, not *of* the world, his life unfolds in the world, but its meaning is not derived from this world. It is essential to analyze our situation, to distinguish "religiosity" from Christianity, to look beyond the surface and to discover the underlying motives in order to proclaim the Gospel in relevant terms, a Gospel which demands transformation for the individual first of all that will produce a gradual cultural change.

It could be, as Vahanian asserts, that "the current eclipse of Christianity is caused by an inevitable accumulation of cultural accessories that will in due time be cast away, especially since the more frequent and unmasking confrontations between Christians and non-Christian cultures will lay bare the decadent aspects of those accessories."[5]

The fate of Christianity is not bound to Western culture, the Gospel is of universal validity and addressed to all men everywhere. Missionaries have long purged Christianity from these superficial accretions and proclaimed Christ successfully in other cultural settings.

1. Eliot, T. S., *Christianity and Culture* (Harcourt, Brace, and World), 1949, p. 87.
2. *Ibid.*, p. 10.
3. *The Secular City, op. cit.*, p. 90.
4. Niebuhr, H. Richard, *Christ and Culture* (New York: Harper and Row), 1956, p. 32.
5. *The Death of God, op. cit.*, pp. 152-153.

appendix B

IN HIS writings Altizer makes frequent reference to Captain Ahab, so vividly portrayed by Melville in *Moby Dick*. Many different interpretations have been given of Moby Dick and it may not be easy to unravel the author's thoughts. Ahab is presented as an "ungodly, god-like man," a 'queer man" not a good one, who appears "sort of sick, and yet he don't look so," a "good man—not a pious, good man...but a swearing good man" who at one time was a little out of his mind. He views himself as demonic "madness maddened."

The white whale represents all the evil in the world; it was the "monomaniac incarnation of all those malicious agencies which some deep men feel eating in them...that intangible malignity which has been from the beginning...all the subtle demonisms of life and thought; all evil, to crazy Ahab, were visibly personified, and made practically assailable in Moby Dick."

The sea became an image of "the ungraspable phantom of life" and the whale a pasteboard mask. " 'If man will strike, strike through the mask! How can the prisoner reach outside except by thrusting through the wall? To me, the white whale is that wall, shoved near to me. Sometimes I think there's naught beyond...be the white whale agent, or be the white whale principal, I will wreak that hate upon him.' " The indefiniteness of the whiteness of the whale "shadows forth the heartless voids and immensities of the universe, and thus stabs us from behind with the thought of annihilation...."[1] Ahab perishes in his attempt.

Is Ahab symbolic of "the true worship of defiance" and does his mad hunt picture the response of faith to the death of God? In this conflict Ahab only succeeeds in bringing destruction upon himself—a solemn warning to those who are gripped by Promethean pride.

Ahab does not appear as a happy man. The optismism

which Altizer would have flow from a knowledge of the death of God is nowhere to be seen. This is grim, moody, a monomaniac, consumed with one grand passion. Aloof, enveloped in intense thought, filled with insufferable anguish, "a chasm seemed opening in him" and a "hell in himself yawned beneath him." Crazy Ahab, sleepless, restless, bent on one supreme purpose—Ahab was not marked by this joyful buoyancy, this elastic cheerfulness which supposedly distinguishes the man who confesses the death of God.

Perhaps radical theologians assume that modern man does not need a message of "good news." Man appears no longer as the image of a transcendent God in their writings, but as the product of a series of particular historical and existential situations. The human creature has become its own creator, an autonomous consciousness existing for itself. The historical and existential situations are presumably unavoidable and no amount of "good news" will create a different situation.

It is characteristic of existential authors that they demand transcendence. Sartre holds the view that transcendence towards the divine is the radical project of human nature, although it cannot be consummated. Jaspers demands a transition from the purely empirical being to being as existence-directed-to-transcendence. Heidegger stresses that transcendence is a vertical direction, related to being and expressed in the relation of being to that-which-is and also in the free relation of man to being.

Theologians who believe that "God is dead" do not seem to demand repentance and faith, and seldom speak of radical transformation. When the atonement is viewed as God's self-annihilation whereby the "alien other" dies, the source of confinement and repression has disappeared and the radical Christians is thereby delivered from guilt. Guilt is seen as "a cosmic state of alienation from a universal energy and life." Naturally, forgiveness becomes a cosmic process of "self-annihilation," starting with God himself. He is the author of the atonement (i.e., of his self-destruction), but also the subject of reconcilation.

The profane Christian follows the same path and undergoes the full experience of pain and darkness, of dying, as a way of transfiguration and rebirth. This view of Altizer has so little in common with the Christian demand for repentance and faith, new birth and transformation, atonement and forgiveness of sin, that Altizer should use altogether non-Christian terms to describe his theories.

1. *Moby-Dick, op. cit.*, pp. 104, 185, 201, 33, 181-182, 212.